DRINKING
FROM THE
GOURD

Writings and Training Methods for Drunken Fist Kung Fu

Published by the Drunken Yoga Group: a small collective of traditional *gong fu* practitioners whose goal is to see the propagation of this rare system. Please eschew piracy and support such small authors so we're able to release future projects. Your honesty and integrity are appreciated.

Taipei, Taiwan R.O.C.
drunkenyoga@gmail.com
drunkenyoga.net

The authors and publisher of this material are not responsible in any manner whatsoever for any injury which may occur through reading or following the instructions in this manual. The activities, physical or otherwise, described in this text may be too strenuous or dangerous for some people, and the reader(s) should consult a physician before engaging in them.

The purpose of this manual is to educate and entertain. The author, editor, translator, publisher or any others involved in the production of this book, have neither liability nor responsibility to any person or entity with respect to any loss or damage caused, or alleged to be caused, directly or indirectly by the information contained in this book.

ISBN: 9798831873122

Independently published

從葫蘆喝好酒

師父領進門，修行在個人

"Teachers open the doors, but you enter by yourself."

- Chinese Proverb

FOREWORD

by Zhang Jing Fa

In the ensuing years since the publication of *The Path of Drunken Boxing*, many have asked about very concrete training methods and routines that can be followed to expedite *zui quan* skill development. Without meeting someone in person, it's nigh impossible to create an adaptive and tailored plan with its necessary tweaks and adjustments, as every individual has unique abilities and drawbacks. That said, it is possible to assemble a general framework of training suggestions and patterns that can help round out some of the jagged edges.

Of course, the training numbers, repetitions, and other parameters suggested throughout these writings can and *should* be adjusted to suit different abilities. One shouldn't overtrain, but know that limits need to be pushed beyond comfort levels to achieve progress. Keeping a journal of what's being worked on assists in formulating a map of where you've been, and where you hope to arrive at next. This is true in early days, as well as years further ahead. I've yet to meet a high-level practitioner of anything that hasn't logged their journey in some way. Keep a journal.

Seek out many teachers with an open, yet critical, mind. Pressure test as much as possible and internalize what works, making it your own and letting it steep deep into your bones and tissues. Don't throw things away, as you may not yet have the discernment to see its value. Having more premium-level martial artists in the world is never a bad thing.

This book has been divided into three the sections of *Jing*, *Qi*, and *Shen*, roughly corresponding with physical training, breath / internal work, and spiritual / character practices, respectively. It's a collection of writings and insights by various practitioners of drunken fist who feel they have some insights to offer—things they wish they'd been able to tell their younger selves—in order to avoid pitfalls and unnecessary stumbling blocks. Along with each writing is a "daily dose", which is a training regimen that can be adapted to fit one's own personal agenda and current martial abilities. Perhaps it can be valuable to you in that regard, or perhaps you're beyond some of these benchmarks, and can use this as a reflection tool for how you overcame similar challenges in your martial growth. Either way, it's good to know there are others challenging themselves along this martial path, seeking betterment and higher personal levels. As previously stated, having more premium-level martial artists in the world is never a bad thing. Train hard.

FOREWORD

by Ma Hao Xing

Welcome to *Drinking from the Gourd*, aka *Long Drinks from the Gourd*, a work that was easier to conceptualize than actually manifest. The idea behind this book was to compile the perspectives and ideas from a variety of practitioners of drunken fist in an attempt to add more discourse to this relatively obscure and misunderstood martial art. What is already a highly-complex art becomes even more complicated when you try to express these ideas via the written word, but if that wasn't enough, I also wanted to include functional input, meaning that I wanted to include actual training regimens and practices that would encapsulate the theories and concepts explained. The latter is tricky, as there really is no "one-size-fits-all" when it comes to training, so things like numbers of repetitions or time spent doing a given exercise cannot be accurately prescribed. Instead, general ranges or guidelines are included, in the hopes that not too much is lost in translation, and each individual has enough experience to ascertain their own customized routine.

None of the training is easy; but you already know that. All of the results are hard fought-for; but you already know that. If anything, much of the information should be somewhat familiar, in which case it should act as a reinforcement for the fact that you're on the right track. New kernels of information can be incorporated into your practice, perhaps being one of the missing ingredients for a breakthrough you've been seeking. Your success in drunken boxing is *OUR* success in drunken boxing, as we're all struggling for betterment in the art, regardless of our current place along the path. Drink up!

Acknowledgments

Special thanks to all of those who contributed their time and expertise to this project. Training methods and insights vary, and while may even seem contradictory at times, they all add to the rich tapestry that is martial arts of Chinese origin. Despite the uphill struggle for preservation of many traditional arts, these contributors all did so with the common goal of propagation and perpetuation of the physical culture skill known as Drunken Boxing. The question posed to them was:

What actual, pragmatic training methods can one follow to learn proper *Zui Quan* skills?

Their generous responses and insights have been included in this book.

Much gratitude to Shifu Neil Ripski of the Red Jade School, whose writings harmonize nicely with many of the training approaches outlined in this text, and have been included to offer his insights and wisdom on the topics.

"We don't rise to the level of our expectations;

we fall to the level of our training."

-Archilochus

DRINKING FROM THE GOURD
- CONTENTS -

精

LONG DRINKS FROM THE GOURD

by Zhang Jing Fa

Many layers of depth are imbibed in the humble calabash or "bottle gourd". Spanning a range of topics such as food, medicine, magic, superstition, utensils, fertility, and music, it's very telling of the interpretive nature of Chinese culture and the ability of people to analyze the characteristics of something as unassuming as a simple HúLú, or gourd. This is, in part, due to how the Chinese language is utilized. Owing to its limited phonetic inventory, homophones – words that sound the same – comprise a large part of the language, resulting in many puns to denote a wide range of communicative tasks, including conveying humor, rhetoric, poetry, or colloquial sayings. In this way, it's very common to find words of the same or similar sounds to denote other meanings, both good and bad.

Mystical beliefs posit that gourd charms ward off evil, as the first syllable in the word *hulu* sounds similar to the words for "blessing" (祜) or "protect" (護), despite being differently written characters and tones. It's also similar to how the word *fulu* (福祿, meaning happiness / rank), is intertwined with the word for gourd, and therefore has the latter considered a lucky symbol in this regard. These are just two examples of how such phonetic associations tie together seemingly disparate objects and phenomena in Chinese language and discourse.

Other beliefs include how *hulu* were considered effective at "trapping" diseases and negative spirits inside, so would be hung in various places to lessen the effects of such phenomena in a household or community. *Fengshui* ideology suggested gourd charms to be kept in close proximity to one's bed following an illness for this reason, the idea being that it resulted in speedier recovery and bolstered vitality. Such believers also thought that keeping such a charm on your person in daily life would protect against encroachments by ghosts and evil spirits. Elderly citizens would frequently carry around and display gourds or gourd charms, as *hulu* were representative of longevity and an extended, fruitful life. Abundance and prosperity are reflected in the ease of growing *hulu*, as they generate quickly and with a plentitude of seeds, which is also the same reason they're associated with fertility and procreation.

Historically, hollowed gourds were common receptacles for keeping water, wine, and medicines, as well as magical potions concocted by *Daoist* adherents and other such mystics or supernatural beings. *Daoist* doctrine also draws parallels between the shape of gourds and the universe, made up of the earth and the heavens, as well as the infinite. They are considered gateways to another universe, and were supposed to be a method of distilling the "elixir of immortality", with red cinnabar and mercury placed in the upper and lower chambers, respectively. Uniting these two, according to such adherents, represented the combination of male and female essences to create life. The gourd's shape has also been a metaphor for beginning and creation, said to resemble a womb. All of these examples demonstrate that the *hulu* has been incorporated into innumerable positive situations and beliefs. That said, they have also been included in many other facets of culture, including stories, legends, and music. Deeply influential literature, such as "Journey to the West" (xī yóu jì – 西遊記), depicts the famed Monkey King (Sun Wukong 孫悟空) outwitting some demons, deceiving them in order to take possession of a magical gourd. Musical instruments fashioned from *hulu* also were a component of popular culture, showing just how pervasive this item is.

Drunken boxers, familiar with the *Daoist* Immortals, know that "Iron Crutch Li", *Li Tie Guai / Tie Guai Li*, possesses a gourd, which is integral to his existence and interactions. Never becoming empty, the *hulu* he carries with him is said to be filled with medicinal substance that cures any ailment, which he uses to administer to the frail and downtrodden. Along with this, his *hulu* has also been depicted as a container for storing his *hun* or soul, and as a shelter for sleeping in. The relevance of these representations become much more apparent the further you take your drunken fist training.

One takeaway symbol for martial artists who practice the drunken arts is seeing the representation of the gourd as part of the process of freeing the body from contaminants and disease. Strengthening the body and spirit is achieved by embracing the healing properties representative of the *hulu*, finding physical, mental, and spiritual balance via exercise, breath control, meditation, sleep, diet, and herbal treatments. It's not uncommon for *gong fu* practitioners in the Drunken Immortals style to keep a medicine gourd of *die da jiu* liniment on hand for healing after a training session. Gourd seeds are planted in the Spring and the vine bears fruit in the Autumn. This directly parallels one's *gong fu* journey, as the best gourds are the ones that are cultivated well and with patience. For a drunken boxer, a gourd is a drinking vessel, a weapon, a medical implement, a meditation visualization, a symbol, and even a guide, all of which actualize throughout different phases along the *Zui Quan* path. The HúLú embodies *yinyang*, and is expressed variously in *jing*, *qi*, and *shen* interpretations, and is interwoven into multiple components of the mindsets and training methodologies contained herein. No matter where you are now along the path of drunken boxing, all *zui quan* practitioners are, in some way, drinking from the gourd.

The CANDLE

Jing   Qi   Shen

THE CANDLE: *Jing, Qi, Shen*

One of my former teachers had a great skill for describing things as simply as possible. Indeed, simple and straightforward were key to his approach to most things. He was fond of recounting a tale of one of his own past masters, and how he lauded one hallmark of intelligence as being the ability to take something extremely complex and then simplify it, "so even a dullard like me could understand."

When posited with a question of how to explain the three treasures—the *sanbao*—he naturally had a way to distill *Jing, Qi,* and *Shen* into a succinct analogy. To see things clearly, he instructed us to think of a candle.

He described it like this: the *Jing* is the tangible physical aspects of the wax and wick, the burning flame is the *Qi,* and the *Shen* is the heat and glow given off. If pressed further, he could go further into details and philosophies behind these terms, but ultimately, as such discourses do, it ended up just *splitting hairs* and being "exercises in logic and philosophizing." He'd also be quick to remind us that time spent daydreaming on abstract concepts was time taken away from practical training. He loved hard training.

However, in the interest of being a bit more thorough, it's important not to overlook the added aspects of pre- and post- heaven categorizations, 先天 (*xiantian*) and 後天 (*houtian*), respectively. The prefix added to terms to denote "pre-heaven" is "*yuan*", meaning "original". This leaves us with 元精 (*yuanjing*), 元氣 (*yuanqi*), and 元神 (*yuanshen*), or "Original *Jing*", "Original *Qi*", and "Original *Shen*". An abridged explanation is the genetic qualities you inherit are *xiantian*, while the *houtian* elements are conditions you can foster and reinforce through diet, lifestyle, environment, and training. The latter is where a deliberate and tested *gong fu* system comes into play.

Jing: What determines how the candle burns is the quality and composition of the wick and wax. Characteristics passed on via parents are part of original *jing*, and compose the "essence" of one's physicality. While it takes a long time to draw from and use up this reserve, it's also difficult, or impossible, to restore. From birth onwards, it's regulation of habits, awareness, and lifestyle that determine the wick's length, and how much wax is consumed by the flame, and overall, the way in which the candle burns and depletes.

Qi: The flame continually burning down the candle is your *qi*. *Qi* in original form starts from the moment you're born, and is expressed daily in energy and vitality. It is restored relatively quickly by means of correct breathing, nutrition, rest, and mindset, but it also diminishes much faster than *jing* does. Just as candles can burn in different ways, so, too, can an individual's *qi*. Some fires are constant and fluid, while others generate smoke or flicker or flare up irregularly. It's apparent how directly this affects the progress at which *jing* is expended, so *qigong* and *neigong* methods to regulate the *qi* and harmonize the flame, lead to what many call "balance".

Shen: The "windows to the soul" immediately display a shine, beginning from the moment you're born. The heat and light emanating from the candle are your *shen*. This naturally hinges upon how the *jing* and *qi* are kept in tune for the duration of life. Imbalance dims and diminishes the flame, while in contrast, strong functioning of all components results in an abundant and radiant soul.

SIMPLY GROUPS

Then again, these labels are just a way of categorizing things to assist memory and dissemination of knowledge. We have to keep in mind that groupings like *jing / qi / shen* are just folktale ways of explaining and codifying complex phenomena. For largely illiterate societies, or oral traditions, having such means of remembering and arranging things makes sense. This is not to say that many hours of academic study have not gone into these phenomena. In fact, quite the opposite. One of the hazards is that many people get caught-up in the over-intellectualization of these terms, rather than putting effort into actual training.

Other qualities ascribed to *Jing-Qi-Shen*, respectively, include, "past, present, future", "combat, fitness, healing", "earth, man, heaven", "*yang*, transition, *yin*", and many others, if you really dig into it. One *thing* can also be all three, depending on purpose. Take, for instance, a knife. It can be a weapon for warfare, used in defense and offense, maiming and killing others. It can be a tool for food preparation for nourishing the body. It can also be a surgeon's implement, used medically in later stages of health recovery. This is an exemplification of "combat, fitness, healing", and it's easy to see how this applies to martial arts training.

Most times, this trifecta is used to explain internal experiences and processes. However, it can also be applied to something like the analysis of an attack. For instance, *jing* is the initial attack by the opponent, the physicality of bridging with someone at the outset of an altercation. *Qi* is the relationship between you and the opponent as you navigate the correct response and implement your own defensive tactics. This would include things like joint manipulations or where you counter-strike. *Shen* is your internal reaction to the attack, the control over your sympathetic nervous system and adrenal dump, as well as the Buddha-nature concept of harm reduction and showing mercy to an opponent appropriately.

In the above example, rather than being strictly about one's internal navigation, it's applying these labels to an event involving another person. Regardless, it still becomes a useful tool for analysis. You can see how it's a simplified model for explaining things, and how each separate part could also be broken down further for examination and study. In the breathing component of the above example, one's breath / *qi* during combat could be further subdivided as follows:

Jing: the physical act of respiration, referring to the diaphragm and physical components of the breathing apparatus.

Qi: Energetically, it's the exchange of oxygen and carbon dioxide and distribution throughout the body creating the relationship between the inside and outside world.

Shen: Spiritually, it's the calming and centering nature of the breath that focuses everything into alignment, leading to deeper spiritual realization when done mindfully and correctly.

Or, at the end of the day, we're all just candles, burning down at our own unique pace, and the best way to spend that time is training *gong fu*.

ZUI QUAN OVERVIEW

Zui Quan Overview
A Drunken Fist *Gong Fu* Essay

When asked what *Zui Quan* really is, it only makes sense to say that it's *everything*. It's everything you think you know about martial arts, and then beyond that, too. It's striking, kicking, throwing, locking, grappling, weapons, medicine, meditation, *qigong*, *neigong*, culture, lore, fanciful tales, misconception, and myths. It's a history of war and turmoil, along with more people starting than finishing. It's about quitters, thugs and madmen, as well as those on the opposite side of the spectrum. It's what you want it to be, but it's also a whole ton of discouragement, and your own misinterpretations shattered. On a basic level, it's one path up the martial arts mountain we climb.

Qin Na and *Shuai*: Locking and Throwing

It goes without saying that a skilled Drunken Fist practitioner needs to be well-versed in many kicks, punches, and blocks. Along with this, it's from a long and rich history of Chinese *qin na* that *gong fu* players get most of their grappling techniques, resulting in a solid arsenal of *Zui Quan* abilities. In fact, a large portion of a skilled practitioner's repertoire incorporates a varied and in-depth grappling element. As such, the Drunken Fist practitioner actually should spend an appropriate amount of time learning techniques such as clinching, throws, joint locks, chokes and strangles. By the time one has advanced enough to truly be doing drunken fist correctly, these types of *qin na* skills should have already been absorbed, practiced, and well understood.

Wrists. A critical component of *zuiquan*, and indeed any well-rounded *gong fu* training, is wrist conditioning and the subsequent wrist strength that results. The hooking, gripping, pressing, striking and piercing of the drunken cup fist hand position by definition requires supple, yet stable, wrist joints. Included in the attack toolbox is the appropriate use of a wide variety of wristlocks, provided the opportunity presents itself or is created. While such locks are a common method in multiple martial arts, their execution in drunken boxing varies, differing from those of many other well-known combat forms. The question is: how?

As a very basic level, these locks naturally must adhere to the geometries laid out by human anatomy, described variously as: supinating / pronating, internally / externally rotating (choose your nomenclature: the human body only moves in so many planes). To simplify: think of up-down, left-right, and diagonals. That being said, add spirals to different aspects of the attack, as well as acupuncture points for an array of pain or control effects, and you've established a formidable arsenal of wrist joint attacks alone. A joint lock is just that: the isolation of a relatively small joint, creating a solidly locked structure that inflicts pain and/or damage. Drunken fist's unique element is the relaxed nature employed, combined with unusual vectors of entry to attack. A good lock is one that is done without the attackee feeling the setup or process, in fact only noticing the rigid finish when it's already deeply set. Often being described as a very "*yin*" or yielding feel, the correct body methods / *shen-fa* of *zui quan* must be worked on and integrated into movement of the self before it can be properly imparted into opponents. Solid *jiben gong, buzhu gong* and *neigong* sets of any valid style should imbibe these within the student. Wrist attacks are just the distal joints of the limb, and equally in-depth analysis can be done as we towards the core of the body.

Elbows. The next "gate" is the elbow, which opens up more avenues for dominance during combat. When learning percussive elbow attacks in the drunken curriculum, the student also is taught elbow locking techniques such as filing, grinding, folding, and pressing, among others. If the joints are systematically attacked, invaded and destroyed, it methodically eliminates the adversary's potential for retaliation. Drunken Fist has a beautiful and unique array of tactics which center upon the manipulation of the elbow joints, usually used in a sequential manner for most effectiveness. It's rare that just one of the joints of the body can be attacked, especially as you progress to fighting more adept adversaries. Combinations, feints, distractions and subtle skills must be woven together into a proper tapestry of attack sequences, often outwardly portrayed as retreat, weakness or fear in the drunken player. Deception is always a valid weapon of wine fist *gong fu*.

Shoulders. In terms of the shoulder as the next "gate", it makes sense that these elements of the limbs are used in a chain of action-reaction. Decisively locking up one leads to seizing of the next one in procession, then the next, and so on, and a skilled practitioner becomes smooth at using these distal joints as a means to grab, control and manipulate the opponent's spine. When you control the person's head or spine, you can effectively control the entire person, generally speaking. Drunken fist, properly applied, allows you to use the protruding radii of the body as levers to maneuver your foe. This is known as "Controlling the diameter" in some martial schools.

Techniques are never used in isolation, so joint locking is implemented part-and-parcel with *shuai jiao*'s throwing and tripping. There is huge value in being adept at executing and defending against proper takedowns. Individual skills may be separated and honed to work on the mechanics, but true skill develops from learning to set them up, chain them together into a proper flow, and use them against a skilled and resisting adversary.

Drunken Fist *Gong Fu* Purpose?

So why do we learn to imitate the drunkard or exude the deep-rooted traits of various drunken Daoist Immortals? There must be advantages to studying Drunken Fist versus learning more orthodox striking styles and a separate grappling style, otherwise why would the *quan* exist? Putting forward such questions is definitely valid, and the answers plumb into differentially shaded depths as well. There are simple answers and complex ones.

Framed simply, there are traditions and long held cultural elements embedded in keeping such styles alive or relevant, and being a bearer of such a torch has appeal. We naturally gravitate towards and thrive on responsibility, so in one regard we're just expressing natural tendencies by being part of a larger martial narrative. We have a responsibility to keep alive traditions that are passed onto us. Bearing responsibility over a long term is a noble trait.

Beyond this, advanced level artists can seek further challenges via intentional embracing of weakness. Training *zui quan* involves challenging your long-held notions of movement, boxing strategy and previously tried-and-true combat methods. It's not easy or readily apparent why one would want to discard years of effort and an orthodox rulebook in order to push further boundaries. It's easy to remain in comfort zones, especially ones that were hard fought for and earned. It's perhaps not for everyone, but there is also always appeal to exploring new territory and pushing boundaries, not to mention attempting a fresh approach when things seem stale.

While definitely a longer, more complex, and traditional path, the way the style is practically trained coalesces into an advanced kaleidoscope of skills, including *qin na*, striking, grappling, submissions, *qigong*, meditation, *neigong*, conditioning, and weapons, and all of these elements are complementary and synergistic. The result is a very complex and complete martial system. Distilled down to very simplistic terms, the multiple approaches are effectively combined as one. That "one", however, is something very unique and hard-won in the vast realm of martial arts, and even within traditional martial arts. It's undeniable that real, combative drunken fist training is hard to come by.

To couch this in a concrete example, think of how a properly executed punch is both a striking attack, angling set up, and balance disruption, while simultaneously "drinking inches" on the opponent as you absorb his limbs, achieving proper grips and positioning for a throw. The deceptive nature imbibed into the *zui quan* art is designed to put the player into pre-strategized ranges and angles that limit the opponent's ability to counter attack, while simultaneously reducing their capacity to defend. In a similar vein, the drunken fist practitioner learns to counter, roll around, absorb and pin in unexpected ways when dealing with an enemy's strike, hence perpetuating its reputation as a deceptive combat art. While many arts have several layers to something like a punch, it's ultimately the body methods, mindsets and strategies of drunken that set it apart.

As cliché as the symbol has become in martial arts or other circles, the *yinyang* or *taijitu* actually perfectly encapsulates the dynamic fluidity of drunken boxing. The constant and consistent ebb and flow of *yinyang* reversal is essentially what the art is, period. Without sounding too vague or mysterious, it's all about appropriateness of technique at a given time. Linear is met with circular, hard with soft, and strength with yielding. While it's easy to espouse such platitudes for any given martial art, it's truly apparent when one witnesses the application of correctly applied wine fist skill. Combine this flexible adaptability with how Drunken Fist artists become proficient at vital targets, acupoint knowledge, and stringing together attack progressions in order to efficiently and effectively dispose of threats, you can see why it's also considered a high-level art form. One of the base practice methods for *zui quan* is "rag doll" training, when a partner pushes and pulls various parts of your body as you stand in place and learn to absorb, reflect, roll and redistribute force. The level of intensity increases as your skill does, and eventually starts to incorporate *zui quan* body dynamics like sloshing, coiling, winding, drinking, expressing, etc. This *yinyang* body method is a prime example of how this theory manifests in this type of boxing.

Like many modern wushu forms in relation to their traditional counterparts, wushu drunken forms tend to be a hollow imitation of what true *zui quan* is actually about. While possibly thrilling and interesting to watch, it really does lack the "engine" that runs the machine. That's not to detract from the athletes that perform such *taolu*, but the essence of what makes it a combat art is lost in such training. "Flowery fists, embroidery kicks" is the common parlance.

"Flowery Fists, Embroidery Kicks"
Kung Fu expression to denote "All style, No substance"

Self-defense?

This is a tricky term, especially given the multitude of schools marketed as such, all purportedly "the best" at this endeavor. Entire volumes can be written on this topic alone, but suffice to say that someone well versed in drunken boxing is amply able to defend oneself. What's problematic is that many people assume it's as simple as a binary classification: you either can or can't defend yourself. Unfortunately, the reality of self-defense is that it's very violent, very stressful, and induces a huge dump of hormones one experiences while under duress. Under such conditions, you're not going to be trying to employ the aesthetic qualities of *zui quan* performance to show off; you're going to need to survive, with as little harm to yourself as possible.

Drunken Fist is a brand of Chinese boxing and self-defense that employs joint locks, pressure points, throws, kicks, and other strikes. This sounds like a generic write up for any combat art, does it not? The fact is, Drunken Fist practitioners learn to counter the techniques of other martial arts as well as common "unskilled" attacks. In fact, its deceptive nature often takes it light years beyond what these types can do. By the time one has advanced enough to properly do *zui quan*, defending oneself with its very effective skill set is a given. Of course, this requires pressure testing, stress scenarios, and lots of mileage with live training. It should be clearly stated that learning a form will not magically impart combat readiness or competency. Also unfortunate in many martial arts schools, is the fact that they lack pressure testing, stress scenarios and training with resisting opponents. Without these in your training, it's extremely unlikely you'll be able to handle yourself in a real attack situation. Wise warriors have said, "you can only fight the way you practice."

Weapons?

When was the last time you were attacked with a spear? Is it common for you to be accosted by a *jian* wielding assailant? If so, your life is substantially different from most others, and quite unique. While traditional weapons no longer crop up as a daily threat, the training of the wide range of traditional *gong fu* and drunken weapons still has viable and applicable purpose. While just a general overview of this art, it should be made clear that traditional weapons such as staff, spear, sword, or others become important training and feedback tools as one advances. They not only amplify and draw attention to areas of deficiency, they also require cognizance of balance, geometries, and *jins* (body energies). When sparring with such weapons, one requires advanced familiarity of distances, angles, and timing which goes beyond the scope of what one achieves with unarmed fighting.

Strategies and Distances?

While Drunken Fist consists of both long- and close-range fighting techniques, the objective of most engagements is to get near enough for a close punch, lock, or throw. Drunken Fist emphasizes spherical motion, non-resisting movements, and ownership of the adversary, controlling his diameter and filling his empty space – spaces deliberately and conscientiously created. Practitioners seek to get advantage by the use of footwork and body positioning to employ leverage, avoiding the use of strength against strength. *Zui Quan* endlessly yields, like a supple willow blowing in a frantic wind. Drunken fighters appear to be playing rather than fighting, which is only further emphasized by its inherently *yin*, relaxed nature.

Ideal Drunken Fist tactics include using footwork and a series of foot / body / hand strikes to bridge the distance with a foe, and can imagine it as being akin to splashing the opponent with wine. Afterward, the player blends with the gaps created, instantaneously controlling the rival's balance by manipulating the head /spine / neck, aiming for takedowns, trips or vicious *qin na*, applying joint manipulations or throws that are suitable for the situation. Drunken Fist – contrary to what many believe – is a comprehensive fighting system, and as the rival's balance has been taken, there are a myriad of techniques used to disable and overcome. Not all drunken boxing schools include fighting methods, so the ones that do are indeed a rare wine.

DRUNKEN FIST: A RARE VINTAGE WITHIN CHINESE MARTIAL ARTS

from discussions with Wang Kunshan

Brief History: Like so many other styles of martial arts, *Zui Quan*'s history and lore are obscured by time and war-ridden cultures that stretch over unstable centuries. With such volatile societies and their penchant to destroy historical records with each succeeding dynasty, it's extremely difficult to say with absolute certainty how a martial art's lineage actually played out. Couple that with a desire for better "marketing" to facilitate popularity of one's school (yes, that has always been a thing), it's easy to see where embellishments prevailed. One only has to look at any different lineage of *gong fu* that trains the Drunkard's Fist to hear completely different tales as to its origins, theories, tactics, and training methods. This is not only true for Drunken Boxing, but for other types of martial arts as well. One of the most famous martial styles to spread around the world is *Wing Chun*, and its various versions of histories, lineage tales, and controversies are many, and well-documented.

That having been said, the legends and tales of a given art are an important part of the micro-culture of a style, and stoke inspiration for practitioners, while at the same time they help to set benchmarks to aim for. Having an ideal to strive for, along with fables to analyze, both encourages us and stimulates our imaginations. In other words, these stories have value beyond simple historical retellings.

Drunken Fist (also known by the names Drunken Boxing, *Zui Quan*, Drunkard's Fist, or Wine Fist) is one of the most unusual and misunderstood types of Chinese martial arts. Though it's basically an unarmed combat technique, Drunken Fist curricula include an array of weapons as part of its study and practice. While the origin of Drunken Fist is definitely rooted in China and its multitudes of combat styles, the real history of its origins has long been a topic of debate. One of the most verifiable references to this style is in the 18th century kung fu manual "Boxing Classic" (拳經; quán jīng), in which Shaolin monks are described as studying and training in Eight Drunken Immortals (醉八仙; zuì bā xiān) boxing. Described as a derivative of ground boxing (地趟拳; dì tàng quán), it was considered quite challenging and high-level. The popularization of

Drunken Fist started in Hong Kong cinema during the 1980s, and has continued to this day in other media, including comics, games, movies, and TV programs, among others. It's from these relatively mainstream sources that most people were exposed to *Zui Quan*, and that's largely where the interest ends. For others, these media sources are actually a starting point for exploration of a fighting style with great depth and skill.

SOME CONCEPTS OF DRUNKEN FIST:

Drunken Fist is based on the overarching principles of Relaxation, Flow, Deception, and High-Level Strategy.

1. The scale of *Fang Song* (Relaxation): Drunken Fist takes the axiom of "not using force against force" in distinct directions. There is a lot that goes into this methodology, however. It's not just about being as loose and floppy as one can be, which ultimately results in little utility. Instead, the idea is to spend hours and hours training in order to examine the spectrum of relaxation available in one's arsenal, and apply the appropriate (and therefore, "correct") level of relaxation required for a given moment. The result is extremely efficient recruitment of full-body energy. This requires, accuracy, appropriate positioning, and the experience to know what these are. Attack is defense, and defense is attack.

2. Flow of Motion: A multitude of martial arts reference the idea of using an opponent's force against himself / herself, even if it's often just paying lip-service to the idea. Actual combative Drunken Fist takes this to a new level altogether, and uses it as one of its core mechanisms and theories of combat. Some of the very fundamental individual and partner drills involve exploring these actions and reactions, and need to be fully integrated in order to advance further. One of the reasons this is considered a very high-level kung fu is that one absolutely must have a solid foundation in order to implement *Zui Quan* effectively and correctly. Awareness of how conventional attacks, defenses, counters, balances, etc. are utilized is needed in order to absorb and flow correctly for momentum changes, coiling and release, sloshing, deception and evasion.

3. Deception: Somewhat contrary to what many may think, deceiving your opponent into thinking you're inebriated is only one small part of what "deception" refers to. In fact, as soon as actual combat happens, any adversary will quickly be aware of this element of the theatrics—"that guy isn't actually drunk...in fact, he's quite dangerous." In actuality, the "deception" refers to the strategies, theories, angles of attack, power generation, and overall confusion that arises from having to deal with these body methods. The relative obscurity of actual drunken combat training enclaves helps maintain this; the less scrutiny of the "secrets", the better. The widespread belief in their ineffectiveness is a great part of the deception.

4. Strategy: Many internal martial arts – such as *Taiji*, *Xingyi*, or *Bagua* – closely study the ways of expressing various *jins* (combative body energies). Largely "internal" in nature, there are similarly many inclusions of various *jins* in proper expression of drunken fist. *Dan tian* sparks movement, which traverses distally to the relaxed and "rubbery" extremities. However, one can have all the subtle and deadly energies in the world, but without a way to correctly implement them, they're effectively useless. Later writings in this text delve into the drunken mindsets, which overlap very clearly with the proper ways of expressing and using *zui quan* in combat settings. Drunken requires relaxation, broken timing, angle changes, height changes, stepping, flow, bridging, clinching, throwing... all with understanding of what conventional fighters would do in a given situation so as to counter it or pre-emptively account for it.

What drives the movement, in terms of methodology? Bobbing, weaving, slipping, head movement and torso contortions? Feigned weakness and imbalance, divided focus? Oddly positioned wrists and fists? All of these combined together sound like a bad idea from a fighter's perspective. The engine that drives the drunken machine must be broken down into its component parts, analyzed, then slowly and systematically built back together again in order to realize its full potential. Learning these composite segments well is what actualizes the drunken fight stratagem.

DRUNKEN FIST FORMS:

So, how do forms come into play in Drunken Fist training? One of the most common complaints among traditional stylists is that most people equate drunken fist with the acrobatic wushu forms seen in tournaments, rather than the actual combative nature of the art. It's often forgotten that actual traditional *Zui Quan* was a high level of training that a student only learned after multiple years of dedication and hard training, and required a very solid foundation upon which to develop correct Drunken skills. Learning forms never means you automatically have somehow absorbed *gong fu*. Forms are a method of cataloging geometries, energies, shapes, and methods, in order to impart an outline of *what still needs to be learned.*

套路

1. *Taolu* / Empty Hand Forms: As with many Chinese combative styles, hand forms show the general philosophy of the movements required to learn and repeat indefinitely. It's also an indicator of shapes and transitions to analyze. Guidance from an experienced teacher will show how the form is a reference for combative techniques (including strikes, kicks, throws, locks, ground fighting, submissions, blocks, movements, evasions, set-ups, timing, power generation / expression), training methods (conditioning, stretching, transitions, *waigong*, movement transitions, power development), and energetics (meditations, structural integrity, *qigong*, *neigong*, breathing, relaxation, health maintenance). Forms should not just be a dance; they should impart layers of study.

武器

2. *Wuqi* / Weapons Training: As a training *tool*, a weapon is an immediate way to amplify gaps, irregularities, and alignment problems, in that it adds both weight and length to one's frame. Hold your arm out in front of you and draw small, consistently sized circles in the air. Now, do the same while holding a lock stick in your hand. The longer and heavier the weapon is, the more difficult the task becomes. Integrate the proper dynamics of each weapon into a form, and it becomes readily apparent where deficiencies exist. Layering this with the added difficulty of the body methods of *zui quan*, wielding a weapon with its distinct and correct parameters becomes high-level *gong fu*, indeed. This is when it's utilized as a training tool. However, weapons need to be used as weapons, or their essence is lost. Finding a school in modern times that actually includes weapons sparring is less and less common, so should be cherished if you have access to one. That said, there are "good" and "bad" ways of doing this type of sparring, as with any type of training. As a general rule, training should be systematic, controlled, and logical in its progression.

Common weapons in drunken fist curriculums include the *dao* / saber, spear, *gun* / staff, *jian* / straight sword, *hulu* / gourd bottle, *guan dao*, sash, fan, and flute. Others may incorporate the fly whisk, ladle, or other instruments and improvised weaponry.

木人樁

3. *Mu Ren Zhong* / Wooden Dummy: *Yong Chun Quan* (Mandarin) / *Wing Chun Kuen* (Cantonese) probably has the most well-known variation of this training type. An approximation of an opponent's torso and limbs is crafted from wooden posts, and is used for repetitive practice of footwork, distancing, angles, and power, as well as a means of physical conditioning. This is true for most styles that integrate the *mu ren zhong* into training, and drunken boxing is no different. One different aspect to *zui quan* is that some styles include mindset or archetype training for the *Zui Ba Xian* / Eight Drunken Immortals into this type of device, trying to replicate the attack methods of each of the drunken deities as one transitions through the form. Much higher level, of course, but worth being aware of if you make it this far into your practice.

雙人套路對練

4. *Shuang Ren Tao Lu Dui Lian* / Two-person sets: Unfortunately, many schools that now include two-person drills often see them reduced to something akin to choreographed dance sets rather than practical combative methods. As an overview, the purpose of these sets is to lay foundations for things such as distance, timing, angles, pressure, footwork, applications, and conditioning. However, if one has already reached a high level in drunken fist, why would foundational skills be a part of the form curriculum? The answer is that they are used for different purposes. All of the above-mentioned skills should already be a solid part of one's repertoire. At this stage, one should have a clear grasp of the difference between *quality* of training and *quantity* of training. A partner set should be used for honing subtle and clever skills, as well as working on flow, reversal of momentum, and minute details of interaction, including breath. This cannot be properly conveyed via text only, and truly requires touching a teacher with real skills. Then, these feelings passed on by the teacher should be (attempted to be) replicated in partner sets and drills. Or, if you're happier dancing, you can just dance. Just remember not to conflate dancing abilities with fighting skills.

JING

PHYSICAL CONDITIONING

JING

Physical conditioning is a core component of *gong fu* training, and becomes even more consequential as you advance. Contrary to what many "internal" practitioners may subscribe to, such physical training is essential to achieving actual softness, longevity, and true skill, even within ostensibly "internal arts". Proper *gong* methods lay the foundation for higher level skills, and without them, the player lacks *gong fu*.

As students, we first learn the overall form of the system – the structures, shapes, strengthening, and primary mentality. This includes finding power in the legs, low standing and holding positions, and moving through low stances. Along with opening the tendons and properly recruiting musculature, the shapes presented to the body teach it how to reshape itself; we teach the body, which in turn teaches itself.

This section of the text is a collection of writings on various *waigong* or external methods to incorporate into your training, if you aren't already doing so. Any good *waigong* practice should include elements that lengthen, stretch, strengthen, activate, coil-uncoil, re-align, and coordinate positions / angles, all within the framework of correct preparation, breathing patterns, mindsets, tension release, and

opening-closing. If you've come far enough in your martial training

to want to take it to the next level of drunken fist, then these

parameters should be quite familiar.

OUT OF BODY, EXPERIENCE:
Zui Quan **Mastery Through Minutiae**

from discussions with Zhu Yingyu

"Checklists" are useful, insofar as they provide concrete goals or steps for training, and I've personally been a fan of this approach since my early days of learning. It's also useful to have such tasks ranked in a hierarchical way, the logic of which comes out as you work your way through the absorption of the skills. "Simpler" skills listed first begin to function as second nature, and thereby require less mental and physical energy to express correctly, or can be fine-tuned even further. A very rudimentary example of this is transitioning through a horse stance: when first learning the mechanics, connections, and internal engines driving the dynamic of the stance, one must meticulously pay attention to the components and attributes. Eventually, such connections and alignments become second nature, and one can use this fluid structure to build other skillsets upon.

水能載舟，亦能覆舟

"Water can both carry and capsize a boat."

One of my teachers was known to say "水能載舟，亦能覆舟" ("*Water can both carry and capsize a boat*", comparable to "*a double-edged sword*"), which encapsulates nicely the nature of the benefits and drawbacks that can be attained when putting our physical and mental training under the microscope. Micro-analyzing a certain aspect of your training can be exactly what you need to level-up, while it conversely could also be the quicksand you get mired in and suffocate under. Having a knowledgeable teacher's watchful eye to guide one through these mazes can be immeasurably valuable, as well as help to avoid frustration and stagnation. That said, the broad-strokes need to be attended to first, without which the finer points are, well...pointless.

1. POSTURE: chest, stomach

So, you've arrived at a martial level deemed reasonable to train *zui quan*. What this means is that you have enough mileage in your martial arts that you now exhibit correct strength and structure, timing and distance, endurance and fortitude. Certain correct alignments should be second nature, and glaring inconsistencies and gaps should be relatively non-existent. Drunken fist training now takes you back to square one, which means you have to-- in a sense-- un-learn much of what you've already absorbed. The standard drunken boxing posture has a sunken / concave chest, rounded back, hips curved forward by way of the tailbone, with a stable center of balance, all done to mask distance and stability. This takes a while to become accustomed to during practice, and even longer during combat. Straying from this unusual postural alignment tends to stiffen the body and cause awkwardness in motions, which is antithetical to this fighting style which stives for extreme *yin*-ness. Locking up into a stiffened posture or reverting to previously instilled habits is one of the hardest aspects to overcome in this style.

2. CENTRAL EQUILIBRIUM, alignments, balance

No matter what awkward posture you find yourself in, there should be a strong sense of balance at all times. This is especially true for the odd positions found throughout drunken fist's classic displays. While training stepping patterns and during fighting training, stop at sudden, random intervals and check to ensure you can maintain your steadiness and equilibrium. At these quick pauses, do a mental checklist of all your structural alignments and positions, and make note of any weak links to later hone.

3. HEAD, balance

"Where the head goes, the body goes"; "control the head, control the fight" (which is true for yourself and your opponent, both physically and mentally). Head movement and evasion is crucial for combative efficacy, but the theatrics should not be expressed at the expense of function and practicality. If this is the case, more training needs to be done to heighten the ruse. Previously mentioned balance also applies to your mind, which should be focused, present, and alert – while appearing not to be so. Maintain a soft gaze, a slight grin, and a wide peripheral vision field. Keep your head in the fight.

4. WAIST, connection

Where is your waist? Drunken schools' reference to the "waist" is the region just below the ribcage and above the hip bone, and is vital for *zui quan* movement. How strong is your core? If the connection between the upper and lower parts of the body is lacking, the *yi* (awareness) rises up and makes the chest of the practitioner top-heavy and imbalanced. Sink into your lower body, thus connecting above and below, keeping your steadiness connected. Rising energy and intent are signs of an inexperienced and mediocre boxer, and leaves one open for multiple attacks. That said, you should be able to feign this very thing while actually being very rooted, thus luring an adversary into a dire situation. This type of training stems from having an iron core and connected waist. If you have yet to discover the benefits of pole shaking, start immediately with a focused practice, as its benefits for body connection are immeasurable.

5. HANDS, limbs

All joints are limber and nimble, tempered like iron through long-term, consistent and intelligent conditioning. Hitting a board with great force multiple times will deaden nerves, enlarge knuckles and indeed create fierce hands. That is, until the *qi* is imbalanced, the disease sets in, and one's limbs are rendered useless. Ultimately, *Gong Fu* is about longevity; self-defense includes defending oneself from disease. Fierce, iron hands can be acquired with proper methodology, and not at the expense of lastingness. Slow and steady wins the race, and is helps along with tested liniments like 跌打酒 / *die da jiu*. Good references already exist in modern times for internal iron palm methods like those passed down via 顧汝章 (Gu Ruzhang) or other established lineages.

Drunken has rounded joints throughout: knuckles, wrists, elbows, shoulders, hips, knees, ankles, toes. Soft, round, and flowing: this is drunken boxing.

6. CORRECT PRACTICE, habits

Practice doesn't make perfect; perfect practice makes perfect. In forms, in stances, in striking practice, in throws, in weapons...there is no cheating. If you're not doing it well, if you're not doing it with full presence and commitment, then you're not doing it at all. Who wins when you give up holding your deep, correct stance? Who wins when you do nine kicks instead of ten on the heavy bag? Who wins when you skip form training today? YOU don't; your opponent does. Only YOU can make yourself succeed. Find your real limits.

Train slow; it's the faster way to progress and success. This is how you achieve great speed, strength, and power.

Drunken fist is hard, don't kid yourself. There's a reason for its rarity, and there's a reason for its relegation to the higher levels of training. 吃苦 : eat bitter.

7. MIND YOUR MIND

The key axiom: 形醉意不醉，步醉心不醉 *Body drunk, mind sober* (literally: *"The shape / form is drunk, the intent is not. The steps are drunk, the heart / mind is not"*)

Don't neglect the deprogramming at the end of a day's session. Don't overlook the importance of standing post *qigong* work, meditations of various sorts, and breathing exercises. Stand, sit, breathe, this is all part of your valuable training. Keep a journal of your ups, downs and breakthroughs, as well as the plateaus. I've never encountered anyone who has regretted such habits.

8. SIMPLE is not basic, it's mastery

Quality over quantity; refine the wine rather than gather more of it. Mastery of any valuable pursuit is found in daily, concerted, and conscientious practice of the fundamentals. Both masters and disciples are on the same path, they're just at different levels of refinement.

"The fight is won or lost far away from witnesses – behind the lines, in the gym, and out there on the road, long before I dance under those lights."

-Muhammad Ali

SLOSHING WINE - HEAVINESS

The Heavy Hands of Drunken Fist

by Lin Guo Jie

每招每勢皆重技擊

"Every move and every situation is a heavy attack"
– Zui Quan Concept

"Sloshing" is the creation of relaxed, heavy power that is omnipresent in drunken fist. It's the recruitment of all the proper components and alignments in your structure and connection that create a soggy, messy, opponent for anyone you're combatively engaged with. Because it's a pervading element of the training, it needs to be trained, indefinitely. Some visualizations of the self are those of being a hollow vessel full of liquid; you're essentially an almost-empty gourd, with a requisite amount of wine swirling around inside. The only issue with this conception, is that it leaves the impression of a solid, inflexible container, when in reality, it's more akin to a wineskin – a soft, pliable bag for holding one's drink. The use of various training tools to demonstrate the actual physics of the liquid's movement should be employed early in one's training, as to correctly impart the nature of such movement. Examples include holding a large jar, barrel, or bucket half full of water to feel the physics of swirling, splashing, and directional changes.

Once one initiates movement (or, better yet, from an external force, has it initiated) in *zui quan*, it really shouldn't stop. Think of a chain reaction. You're the half-full vessel being tossed around in a massive storm. Momentum is movement, which is power. The weight of the sloshing "wine" should carry you, as you need to plunge through space with full weight and structure behind strikes. Drunken boxing "hits" are not the same ideation as in other arts; they are just a part of your body moving heavily through space, intercepting and knocking whatever is in the pathway. Collisions are incidental. This mindset is challenging to achieve, but is necessary for higher levels of execution: you're not actually "fighting", in the orthodox sense, you're just drunkenly moving in space. This can be fueled by various mindsets, such as playfulness, near-sobriety, Eight Immortals archetypes, etc., but this axiom generally holds true.

Further to this, all components of the body are valid weapons, and should be trained as such. Knees, hips, shoulders, elbows-- are all driven by sloshing. When starting out, this should be really exaggerated and obvious, to really get the feel for the mechanism-the sloppier, looser, and messier the better. One teacher said it best: "Don't discriminate between a movement that doesn't have any contact, and one that does. Release the idea of 'fighting', it tenses the body too much. Just hurtle heavily through space."

A heavy bag is a good feedback mechanism for these things, but definitely requires the caveat of starting small and building up. There is an immediate response by the bag / body when something is done incorrectly, and there's not much utility in beating up your own precious joints. Words of wisdom: you'll miss your knees and shoulders when you're older. Heavy bags can take the repeated impacts of your full body weight that a training partner can't, and afford you the opportunity to explore the spectrum of heaviness juxtaposed over the multiple parts of your body and structural alignments. In other words, hit the bag a lot, with all parts of your body, while standing in all manner of different stances, angles, positions, and distances.

Commence motion from your *dantian*, swirling it around in circles. If you're not familiar with the *jibengong* or *fuhugongfa* of drunken, it generally includes various swirling and shaking as driven from this central cog. Really FEEL the wine as it churns in your empty body, and then feel how you can move this heavy liquid into individual body parts as you stagger around the room. Move it into arms, legs, various parts of the torso, etc. This should be thoroughly explored before ever attempting to hit pads, a heavy bag, or any training equipment.

DAILY DOSE:

As a huge proponent of the "bell curve" idea, I think it's always best to start and end in a more reserved fashion, while the middle, or "peak", of the curve is as loose and "drunk" as possible. As an example, a 20-minute session is broken down like this: 5 minutes of stumbling and sloshing around, lightly striking the heavy bag, ramping up to the middle section, which is 10 minutes of intense drunken sloshing and heavy bag strikes, followed by 5 minutes of cooldown, light sloshing and dialing things down again. Depending on your timetable, adjust these proportions accordingly.

1-2-1   2-4-2   3-6-3   4-8-4

CORE EXPECTATIONS
Rocking and Swaying of Drunken Fist

from discussions with Wei Laoshi

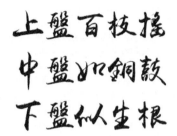

-Drunken Fist Saying

One drunken fist adage states: *"the upper section shakes like 100 branches, the middle section shakes like a bronze drum, and the lower section roots it all."* (above)

Getting the wording right ensures correct understanding. Getting the understanding right ensures correct practice. Correct practice yields good results; good wine. Starting by defining anatomy, we'll denote three different *dantians*, as upper, middle, and lower, corresponding with the head, the chest, and the lower abdomen, respectively. These locales are simply focal points to put your attention as you train: places to put your mind in order to fully grasp how the body is locomoting, and where they are in relation to your overall balance. Correct drilling requires the ability to focus on and isolate movement in each of these three areas, so time spent initially just randomly moving around and mindfully focusing on just one *dantian* at a time is time well spent.

擺和前俯

ROCKING & SWAYING

To train drunken fist, you need massive amounts of time invested into both rocking and swaying. Simplified, "Rocking" means moving the hips, while "Swaying" means moving the head.

DAILY DOSE DRILLS:

WARM UP: Upper and lower *dantian* remain in relative space, and the middle *dantian* rotates in circles. It's usually easiest to start with "sliding" side to side, then work up to making circles in both directions, getting gradually larger as the practice becomes more ingrained.

ROCKING: For the drill, keep your head in relative space, while your hips move around in circles as you take steps. The upper *dantian* is the anchor point around which all movement takes place.

SWAYING: For the drill, you keep your hips in relative space, while your head makes large, circular pathways. You're still stepping, but limit this to small circles so your hips can remain in their limited orbit.

DRILL THREE: Keep the middle *dantian* as the anchor point, while moving both upper and lower *dantians* in circular trajectories as you step in circles. The drills naturally get progressively harder as you advance and begin to incorporate more and more motions and components, such as deliberate and smooth hand / foot movements.

ADDED NOTES: For ALL of these exercises, explore ALL boundaries of your motion, including stepping sizes, speed, directions, and timing, but especially push the envelope in terms of balance. Find the pinnacle reach of your balance, and always try to see where the breaking point is. Over time, this develops noticeably. Only once you're comfortable with the practices should you incorporate weights. Hold something like a weighted bag to your chest, and see how it impacts your momentum and other boundaries. We used to train with sacks of rice from the canteen, hugged to our chests as we did rocking and swaying training. Feel how the added weight changes the dynamic, moves your mass, and adjusts your sense of balance.

搾轉

COIL & UNCOIL the Body's Spring

While the nature of spirals opens up the possibility of this coil-uncoil dynamic in many anatomical locations, the main area to consider is the body's core. The space between the ribs and the pelvic bone has a characteristic to strongly visualize: upon being distended, twisted, or misshapen, it always wants to return to its original position. Once set in motion, there is always a degree of contraction-expansion, uncoil-recoil that is happening. Put another way, in this mechanism exists potential and kinetic energy that are constantly and continuously converted into each other.

This anatomical region seeks continual homeostasis; "it just wants to maintain its shape." When twisted, it wants to un-twist; when compacted, it wants to expand again. The energy created in this process is RELEASED, guided into relevant and useful channels in multiple directions and *jins* (energies). While training these methods, the appearance is that of looseness and ragged sloppiness, while in reality the motions are being driven and powered by this kinetic energy. Explore the feeling of this compaction-expand and coil-uncoil while doing the stepping drills. Adding to that, explore this feeling along a spectrum of extremes: sometimes it's a huge wave of energy created, while other times it's much more subtle.

Drunken standing work is divided into two types: static and moving. The static methods have strength training, *mabu*, and knee-lifting methods; Moving practice has twisting methods, as well as swaying methods, among others. One trait of the standing work is that the heel is pulled off the ground while the sole of the foot remains. This refers to the method incorporated into rocking and swaying drills, whereby the practitioner circles around the ridges of the foot while moving the *dantians*, keeping root with minimal ground contact.

HEALTH

A more active waist, hips, abdomen, and crotch drive the flow within the meridians, which has the effect of health and disease prevention. One integral aspect is maintaining the hip joint: its activity, range of motion, and flexibility. This is achieved via stretching, internal work, rotation, and balance of musculature. Adding more movement in this area draws blood down and strengthens the body overall. Work on your base.

As a general axiom for health endeavors, one must pay attention to the upper and lower, inside and outside, stretching, as well as tension between balance and harmony of the mind. Always notice the reconciliation of breath, and the process of this conversion. Breathe deep into the lower *dantian* – the lower section of the gourd – while engaging in these practices. Keep all areas of the hollow gourd-body well-oxygenated.

Time for Rest, Time for Wrist

by Li Xiaotang

"Learn the rules like a pro, so you can break them like an artist."
-Pablo Picasso

"Your wrists are weak." I remember these words from my teacher clearly, not because it was a bruise to my ego, but because it gave a very clear directive for something to improve upon. Oftentimes feedback can be vague, along the lines of "relax", which can mean any number of things to different ears. "Weak" to "strong" is clear.

PUSH AWAY: This observation put me on the path of correction. I started with regular pushups, slowly, held at low points. Next, was fingertip pushups. Then, moved onto knuckle pushups. This was followed by cup fist push-ups. Then, rotating between all of them: cup fist, to knuckles, to fingers, to palms (x 2), to fingers, to knuckles, to cup fists. Each set resulted in eight pushups, along with a range of surfaces and arm structures being worked on. These are skills that should be ramped up to, so if you need to keep your knees on the ground while starting out, that's fine. If you need to eliminate one of the pushup types, do so. Slowly, slowly, slowly...add elements back in until you're incorporating the complete set.

Following that, begin to increase your repetitions of the set. Slow is fast; consistency in training beats fluctuation. Over time, you can reduce the number of fingers used for the finger pushups as well.

DAILY DOSE: You can never really have too many pushups in your life, can you? Start with one set per day, and evaluate the body's reaction in the following days. If you have no adverse effects, increase the set numbers over time. Aim for ten sets daily.

cup fist – knuckles – fingers – palms –
palms – fingers– knuckles –cup fist

STICK PLAY: Rotating a staff. Using various lengths of wood (or a long staff grasped at various sections), this was something I actually started doing with immediate effects. The trick was not to overdo it, actually. It was really tempting to always try for a longer staff or more weight rather than follow a gradual improvement curve. However, any time I jumped ahead, it always resulted in regression. Lesson learned: going slow is faster. This should be done from various hand and arm positions for best results: a) Hold your hand at chamber and move the distal end of the staff in large circles. b) Bend at the elbow with your hand in front making circles. c) Extend your arm in front to shoulder height and do the same. d) Extend your arm to the side and trace the circles. The challenge for all of these is to ensure your shoulder girdle and joints are not in odd, pinched positions that can result in damage. A longer, heavier stick naturally increases the challenge. Try to maintain uniform circles, not haphazard, messy orbits. Eventually, weights can be added to the staff. One held in each hand simultaneously? Of course.

Ultimately, you want to be engaging your entire connected structure to express motion in the stick, all drawn towards and expressing from your *dantian*. Your wrists will bear the brunt of the drill, but the entire body works out. If you're not sweating and sore from a session with the staves, you need to increase the challenge.

DAILY DOSE: As described above, choose one of the positions, and start with doing ten clockwise and ten counter-clockwise for each hand. Large, consistent, slow, circles. Observe the effects. Repeat. Any types of strain clearly means you've done too much.

A LENGTH OF ROPE: A rope strung over a chin-up bar gripped by both hands is another useful tool. Lie flat on the ground, holding each end of the rope and lift yourself off the ground, like a reverse body weight row / inverted row. The difference is, focus on the spiral twists of the wrists as you lift, almost akin to doing a double corkscrew punch. Pull as far back to chamber as you can, and over-extend the twist on the "punches". The more wrist turning, the better. The additional benefit is the core and full-body workout, which is also great for *zui quan*.

DAILY DOSE: You can never really have too many rows in your life, can you? Start with one set per day, and evaluate the body's reaction in the following days. If you have no adverse effects, increase the set numbers over time. These are a great counter movement for balancing pushups.

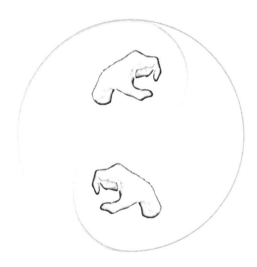

Broken Wrists & Dreams
Use of the Cup Fist in Drunken Boxing
by Shifu Neil Ripski

This is a common question about the cup fist, how does it work for impact? First thing to remember is that the shape of the hand can be changed just before the moment of impact, so the actual hand shape could be a fist or palm or really any martial hand method that is appropriate for the strike being delivered. However, the cup fist is also useful itself for striking and shows us important ideas in drunken boxing overall. But first off to answer the question of how power is delivered through the cup shape.

The cup shape should see the wrist held at a forty-five-degree angle to the long bones of the forearm (radius and ulna) creating an arched shape from the knuckles of the hand through to the long bones. The arch is a powerful structure and so long as the power travels along the curve of the arch it can handle basically anything your body can generate to put through it. The main mistake people make here though is thinking that the strike is straight ahead with a bent wrist, which would of course collapse and break on impact. The strikes themselves when using the cup fist are curved as well, moving in a gentle curve that is somewhat hard to perceive by the opponent and lends itself to slipping past interceptions like blocking methods. It also then delivers the power into the body of the opponent on this curve which is usual for the body to deal with as it tends to "cut off" a piece of the body rather than driving directly through the *motherline* or centerline (*Chong Mai*) of the body as most martial striking methods attempt to do. This turns the opponent from the power of the strike effectively controlling their torso movement through our hit and gives us something to take advantage of. To be able to actually strike with the cup fist requires actually hitting something, over and over like a heavy or sand bag to find the angle of the arch and the appropriate angle of the punch itself to match it.

But this is still only a hand shape and its purpose is deeper than all that. It points at the nature of drunken boxing itself. Many times, I have been asked this question about the use of the cup fist and it shows that it is not simple to understand, it is deceiving even the people who are training the style themselves. Drunken boxing is so deceptive it even lies to us the people trying to understand it. The idea of deception is of course well known in the drunken system but it seems few can be more specific than that it is meant to be deceitful. One needs to try to ask how it is deceiving others? How is it deceiving me? What does deception mean?

At a deeper level the bent wrist implies frailty. This is obvious by the questions about the shape in the first place "I will break my wrist if I punch like that!" this means that seeing and trying to understand the shape as a student it still makes you feel like it is weak and useless, exactly what we want an opponent to think. The lie here is not that we are drunken an unable to defend ourselves (you were sober a moment ago) but that we are unskilled, stupid and doing a useless method. This changes the opponent's level of confidence and allows them to not understand and underestimate the drunken boxer. Secondly the ability to actually use the shape to deliver power shows us that we are to train ourselves to deliver force from strange and seemingly weak positions. If you have ever seen most drunken forms they appear strong, straight and powerful with a little stumbling and rolling thrown in. Not deceptive at all, not on a psychological level nor a physical one. If the practitioner obviously knows kung fu and has structure and line and power he has already missed the ideal of the system he is imitating. It is a bag of tricks instead of a deeply understood method of martial arts. If you do not appear weak you are missing the point.

"This is why we should not abandon the ideals of what we study, thinking ourselves able to simply adjust them to suit our own needs."

Drunken is about taking the weakest positions and understanding them, knowing what balance really is and what its limits are, knowing how to break the "rules" of orthodox martial methods and still retain structure and power. This is why we should not abandon the ideals of what we study, thinking ourselves able to simply adjust them to suit our own needs. This shows a narrow mindedness in our training and an overconfidence in our abilities. The methods are there for a reason, a reason most likely not easy to understand, reasons passed down through generations who trained more years than you have yet lived, what makes you think you know better? I would argue here the often quoted "Take what is useful, reject what is useless", who are you to say what is useless? How many decades have you trained to understand what the art is trying to teach you? Surely you should give it the attention your teachers and generations of teachers before you did before making such judgments. Do not fall into the trap of egoism and knowing better before really understanding what the art is about. Drunken is one of the most advanced and difficult forms of Chinese Martial Arts, this is often said and thrown around in martial culture. If indeed it is an "advanced" system then do not expect it to come easily. I have told my students many times that it took me at least seven years before I started to actually be able to understand it enough to use it in combat and now twenty years in to my drunken training, I am still amazed at how well it is designed, its depth of understanding and its power as a martial art. There are many, many other methods that are simpler to understand and use but fast food is not for everyone. Savor it.

STRONG HANDS, STRONG NECK

from discussions with Zhang Jing Fa & Li Xiaotang

"Without strong hands, you don't have *gong fu*". Quite clearly, I remember one of my teachers saying this. It isn't just in reference to the impact force of fist and palm strikes, or of being able to solidly grip and hold things. It also includes the proper tempering of the tendons and sinews down through the arms and into the fingertips. So how does one ensure this type of strength? Just like most other types of *gong*, it's about proper time and effort. The operative word is "proper".

PUSH-UPS: A good, quantifiable starting point is doing fingertip pushups, which allows for very obvious metrics as to how many repetitions you can do, and on how many fingers (the idea being to gradually reduce to fewer digits being used for the exercise. The important word here is "gradually").

IN A PINCH: The pinching dynamic that exists by having opposable thumbs is a very useful area to strengthen. One classic drill for us was gripping wide-mouthed jars / pots as we walked around the training space, into which we'd gradually add pebbles for weight. Two ways to count progress were either by time or by number of laps with each incrementally added stone. Regardless, the soreness in the fingers and forearms was real, and the consequences for dropped and broken jars was, too. Anyone trying to skip steps and jump to a weight beyond their capabilities was rewarded with having to pay for new clay pots as well as doing fingertip pushups. Paradoxically, *gradual* progress is *faster* progress. Mixing this "pinch" approach up could be achieved by using weight plates held between the thumb and forefinger, which is an equally "grippy" method.

"**Paradoxically,** *gradual* **progress is** *faster* **progress.**"

EXPAND: What is often forgotten by people working on compressive grip training is the opposite, expansive methods to find balance. Elastic bands wrapped around the fingertips and repetitively stretched outwards remedies this. It's simple, and can be done almost anywhere or anytime, even while waiting for a bus. Another option is having a bucket of mung beans, inserting the crane-beaked hand into them completely, then opening the fingers widely, repetitively. Being immersed in beans offers fingers a subtle resistance that works them well if done for multiple repetitions. Pre-training hands and beans should be kept dry to assist hygiene and avoid molding. Some sources posit that the slow powdering of the mung beans from being shifted over time acts as a medicinal tonic for the finger joints and sinews.

HANG AROUND THE BAR: No, not the drinking kind. Having a chin-up bar is useful for upper body strength, but also to hang on. Work your way up to longer times, or even add weights to the body / legs. Simply hanging and supporting your own body weight by your finger strength is harder than it sounds. To work another range of various muscle groups, put a short length of rope over the bar, and hang from it, gripping the ends in a spiral-type grip. Feel the spiraling all down through the forearms as well.

CARRY: Carrying heavy objects with a hooking grip is yet another practical drill. Get a bucket with a handle, and fill it with gravel to make it effectively challenging. Arm downwards and straight at your side, carry the bucket for laps, paying attention to your posture and entire shoulder girdle as you do so. Make sure your entire shoulder and carrying apparatus is engaged and in proper alignment. If you have two identical buckets, carry one in each hand for a variation of this.

WORK THE NECK

"Without a strong neck, *gong fu* is weak." Quite clearly, I remember this wisdom from my teacher as well. He was very fond of, and adept at, getting grips around an opponent's neck, effectively gripping the entire spinal column and being able to direct the conclusion of the bout. The neck, as well as all of the spinal erector muscles all play such a vital role in posture and structural function, logic dictates that compromising elements of this anatomical set in an adversary would be combatively strategic, and fortifying the same for oneself would be extremely beneficial. So, how does one develop this type of strength? As before, it's about proper time and effort. Again, the operative words being "proper" and "effort".

STRETCH: Simplifying, the pathways of movement are forward-backward, side to side, and diagonals, as well as having the neck's ability to rotate. Lots to work with. Begin with stretching in these various capacities: 1. Looking down, looking up. 2. Tilt to each side, using the same-side hand to gently the ear down towards the shoulder. 3. Turn, looking left to right. 4. Stand with your back to the wall and tuck your chin in, drawing your head skywards. 5. Turn your head 45 degrees to the left, use your left hand to grip the crown of your head, and stretch your neck down, forwards, diagonally (repeat on the right). These are standard stretches that should be second nature.

LIGHTLY ENGAGE MUSCULATURE: 1. Lie face down with your arms touching your sides. Repeatedly raise your head only, looking in front of you. 2. On your hands and knees, do the same motion, raising your head, looking down, then looking up again.

RESIST: Next, add some resistance. 1. Left palm against the left side of your head, without turning or bending, push your head against your resisting hand for ten seconds, then repeat on the other side. 2. Fingers clasped and put against the forehead, push forward with your head as you resist with your hands. 3. Repeat, this time with your hands clasped behind your head. You determine the amount of resistance, so listen to your body and challenge yourself, without overdoing it.

HARNESS: If you can perform the above with no adverse effects, then begin to add weight into the equation. Conveniently, it's quite

 easy to find inexpensive head harnesses that are designed for neck workouts. It's also quite easy to make one with various materials, just be sure that it's reinforced enough to avoid snapping. Start with light weights, and work up to more, gradually. Gradually. 1. Sit on the edge of a chair with the harness on your head and weights dangling in front while you raise and lower your head, up and down. 2. Lie on the edge of a bench or bed, face down, and do the same: up and down. 3. Lie on your side: up and down. 4. Lie face up: up and down. Cover all directions and planes of motion.

WEIGHT: No harness? No problem. Weight plates, or even heavy books work fine. 1. Lie face down with your head hanging off the side of a bench or bed, and hold the weight on the back of your head: raise and lower, up and down. 2. Flip over, belly down, and do the same, this time with the weights on your forehead. 3. Same on the side, weight on the side opposite to the ground. As above, cover all directions and planes of motion.

PAIR WORK: Our teacher would pair us up, and have A lie on the floor face up, while partner B would stand straddling over him, bent forward at the waist so we were basically eye to eye. Partner A would clasp fingers and wrap around B's neck, effectively becoming the weight for B's workout. Up and down, as well as up and down on a diagonal plane. Definitely something to work up to, and a workout that varies according to your partner's size and weight. It adds interaction into the mix, as well as the tactile element of what it feels like to have a grown human's dead weight grasping around your neck.

These, or other similar methods have been examined in other resources and books, but they all echo the same sentiment: keeping hands, tendons, body connections and fascia well-tuned pays dividends in terms of overall martial skills, regardless of your chosen style or lineage. This type of 力 (li – physical strength) combined with internal connections and methods, results in power that is hard to deal with for any opponent.

DAILY DOSE: Begin with ten-second- or ten-times repetitions, integrating them into your daily routine. Overdoing it will be abundantly clear, so work in increments. Add further sets as you progress. Work all ranges of motion, and don't work injuries.

THREE SHOTS
Water Training –Liquid Movement
by Lin Guo Jie

You need to move slowly, methodically, and effortfully, as though you were immersed neck-deep in a viscous liquid like honey. In all likelihood, you've had experience trying to walk through water of various depths, or tried moving your limbs while immersed in a pool, and this is the same dynamic that underscores this training. While motions are heavy and done with resistance, it's important to remain as relaxed as possible while engaging your musculature. Ultimately, you're seeking the balance point of using as little musculature as possible to achieve body movement. The slowed-down nature of the environment allows you to examine the pathways and connections of motions, ensuring you're following proper trajectories, expressing valid shapes, keeping correct balances, and breathing rhythmically.

While this methodology can and should be done with multiple various aspects of one's *gong fu* and *zui quan*, for this discussion we'll be focusing on what is known as the "Three Cannons". Keep in mind that this type of exploration can be applied to any of your training, but it's vital to have a list of parameters ahead of time, as well as empirical ways of ensuring you're remaining on task. For the latter, it helps to have a teacher, or at least an experienced training partner, who can point out when you stray from the agenda.

Trajectories, body connections and correct energies for each strike can really be delved into if slowed down and examined carefully. This is not dynamic tension training in the sense that you're using extreme contraction to slow your own movements. Rather, it's keeping muscles engaged and relaxed so that you feel them working, but you're not shaking or breathless. This will be a workout, but it should be quite evenly paced. For those keeping track: you will gain strength, and you will improve your cardio. However, these are peripheral benefits.

For those unfamiliar with the three cannons, it's simply three strikes done in succession repetitively. However, what's often overlooked in training of this nature is the SUBSTANCE behind the training; quality over quantity is paramount. The physical description of the set is outlined in detail by Shifu Ripski below:

Three Cannons 三大砲 / by Shifu Neil Ripski

Three Cannons is the simplest of the secret exercises and is usually the one where a student should start. The three movements are simple in appearance: a low splitting cup strike, a standing uppercut and then a dropping low cup punch. Each of the three stages has a few things to put into play when training.

First Cannon 第一炮 : The two hands are moving in different ways in this first movement. The hand moving forward should be driven directly forward from the movement of the torso at the level of the player's own heart. The rear hand is swinging in a horizontal arc backwards like a back fist. This creates a splitting force between the two strikes by allowing the torso to turn naturally and yet express the force in two different directions with two different *jins* or "energies". It is important that each of the hands is travelling in its preset arc to create not only splitting force, but also a forward and sideways force driven from the shoulders.

While the legs are twisting into the "running step" shape, *dantian* is not only turning as the driving force of the body, but is also dropping lower towards the earth. Ideally this done with a great deal of relaxation will result in "dropping force", adding the weight of the body into the strikes.

Second Cannon 第二炮 : Turning *dantian* in the reverse direction from the first cannon will affect all the parts of the body. This should be trained to pull the leg inwards towards the body from the previous "running step" stance. Movements must remain coordinated and the leg should not be moved without the feeling of the torso rotation (*dantian*) pulling the leg in. This is to train inwards power in between the legs used for sweeping and resisting sweeps. The front hand that struck forward in the first cannon is pulled backwards and upwards into the "drinking from the cup" posture. It should be positioned above the temple of the player at a forty-five-degree angle. The most important thing to remember for this hand, however, is that the power moves backwards through the elbow. Although it appears as a high block similar to something from an orthodox style of martial arts, its power is moving backwards primarily and not upwards. The uplifting of the arm is a result from the standing up into the one-legged crane stance more so than anything the arm itself is doing. A good way to accomplish the correct power or "line of drive" is to imagine elbowing someone behind you downwards.

The formerly rear hand from the first cannon turns into an uppercut strike with the cup fist. As always this must be a result of the turning of the dantian (torso/hips/kua). This uppercut must also be spiraling as it rises with an outward turning. This is known as a "positive" spiral when the thumb moves outward and upward into a "thumbs up" position. This spiraling force needs to be present for this part of the movement to be correct, creating upwards drilling force.

Third Cannon 第三砲 : The most difficult of the movements is the third cannon. The previously uplifted arm in the second cannon that was "elbow striking behind" now drops down in front of the body with a spiraling, downwards strike. The most common mistake when performing this is to "drop" the arm as though setting it on a table top rather than drilling it downward like driving it through the lower torso of an opponent. This is usually an issue with the beginning of the movement, dropping the wrist directly downward before initiating the turning of the body (dantian) and then driving its force downward and forward into the opponent. The hand travelling backwards to the waist should be thought of as an elbow strike behind you driving the power generated by the waist through the elbow.

Lastly all three of the strikes in the exercise should pass through the same space, an area about the size of a person's chest as though you were striking at the heart of an opponent with all three cannons. It is also extremely important to note how little the arms are actually moving throughout the exercise, they move as a result of the torso turning and the arms themselves simply allow that movement to express force through them as they take shape.

The waist moves and creates the force while the arms simply take shapes to express that force through them.

Once you have the gross physical patterns worked out on both sides, you can start examining different layered aspects of training while immersed neck-deep in water, putting in the requisite multiple repetitions.

While this water training can and should be done with many other components of (form) training, using the three cannons to start off with works well for many reasons. First of all, the actual physical and internal dynamics (outlined above) are extremely important for *zui quan* practice in general. Keeping focused on three core – yet different – movements is a powerful tool if trained mindfully. Just these three motions alone have a huge amount of material one can hone, indefinitely. Once the large, gross movements are done in a coordinated fashion, more and more subtlety can be included. Water, by its nature, is denser than air, so it amplifies certain qualities we can pay attention to while training. Some of the aspects to explore include:

1. PRESSURE: Feel "where" the water is resisting your limbs and body. As an example: doing a twisting punch underwater, one can obviously feel the water "pushing back" as you thrust forward. Along with this, there is resistance in a spiral up the arm as it moves through the water. The entire length of the limb "scrapes" through the liquid, and depending on the amount of force used, the environment "shudders" upon release. Given that you're not just striking with your arm, there should be many other areas of contact and motion on your body.

2. BODY: Use only your torso to do all the motions, letting your arms hang limply at your sides, studying how the water is shifted and sloshes while doing so. Make all movement originate from the lower *dantian* very consciously. In effect, you're still "punching", but without using your arms; the only movement happening is core-driven, using the body. This should really emphasize how to drive your strikes and coordinate your body during the Three Cannons set.

3. DRIFT: Move once, then feel where the currents push you. For instance, after doing a single straight punch towards the front, the water is going to react in splashes, swirls, and currents all around you, and you should sit and "feel" where this movement of water carries you. If you lightly stirred a glass of water, then put a single drop of black ink into it, you'd see the dark ink swirl and assimilate into the spinning current. This is to be *you*, on a larger scale. Explore how this dynamic of the water can "push" you into the next move of the Three Cannons set. There's no need to rush from one movement into the next; rather, paradoxically, the slowest way often leads to the fastest progress.

4. RESPIRATION: Really notice your breathing. The slight, constant pressure of the water all around you is a physical reminder of keeping a well-paced respiration pattern. You'll come to notice small areas where you unconsciously hold your breath or speed up your breathing pace. Awareness is the first step to change, so the water becomes a tool for finding these gaps.

KICKING, HITTING & SCREAMING

Some SPEED with your Drinks

from discussions with Guo Tian Rui

拳法剛柔相濟，快速靈活，
以迅雷不及掩耳的速度把對方擊敗

*"The boxing method harmonizes strength and softness, speed and nimbleness;
it defeats opponents at lightning speed."*

-Drunken Fist Saying

This drill is often labeled as counterintuitive to our normal boxing standards. Usually, we seek full-body connection, as this is paramount to many positive outcomes, including health, power, speed, and overall effectiveness. However, this practice is one of isolating segments of our body, honing small, distinct elements before we add them into the larger machine. This is "greasing the minor gears".

Stand in a drunken boxing stance. In this drill, contrary to working on entire body connection and power, we're only working on the movement in the shoulder and arm, so there will be no motion in the rest of the body. The idea is to throw fifty simple strikes, each thrust aiming to be faster than the previous one, generating all motion and power from the musculature in the shoulder and the arm. You want to get to the target and retract as fast as possible. By isolating these muscle groups, you're ensuring they fire in correct sequence and range, which can then be added to full body mechanisms later on.

It's important to do these drills without hitting anything like a bag or pads, as you're developing the internal awareness and proprioception needed for when you start actually employing the methods for hitting things. The actuality of hitting something gives a tactile and obvious sign to retract, so it's a different skillset being worked on.

From this, you're aspiring to having correct timing; if you're retracting too soon, you're pulling your punches, and not getting enough extension and range. If you pull back too late, your limb is left extended and vulnerable, exposing your body, joints, and head, dropping your recoiling punch, ultimately showing lazy technique. Finding this range takes a bit of trial and error, but quite quickly you'll discover what your distancing is, and your body mechanics will offer feedback.

DAILY DOSE:

Start with fifty jabs, punching on target with your leading arm from your drunkard's stance. Make sure you're consistent with your aim, extension, retraction, and goal to achieve increased velocity with each strike.

Continue by doing fifty crosses, firing the strikes with your rear hand. Before doing so, actual turn your hips as you would when employing your whole body for the punch, but leave them locked in place. This ensures that you're at the end of range for your body motion, and you'll just be using your arm. Given the nature of the drunken stance, strikes are done slightly diagonally when aiming for the opponent's face. As with the lead-hand punches, try to get each subsequent strike faster than the previous one.

When starting out, it's easier to keep hands closed into conventional fists, focusing on the arm components only. As you become more comfortable with the exercises, you can work on keeping your hands in cup fists when retracted, tightening them into regular fists as you extend and strike.

TIPS FOR PUNCHES:

1. STAY LOOSE AND RELAXED: Fire some shots, then recalibrate to find areas of tension.

2. DON'T TELEGRAPH: Don't rock, cock, or bounce.

3. CUT THE DISTANCE: Closer to target means less distance to travel, therefore it can arrive faster (closer "firing point"). This is part of the deception of *zui quan*. Getting correct stances and angles builds this into the overall body of the drunken fighter. Play with the stepping and distances to find deceptive and closer firing points.

STUMBLING AROUND LIKE A FOOL

by Zhang Jing Fa

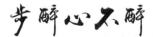

"Drunken steps, sober mind"
-Drunken Boxing Precept

Footwork wins the fight. Once you have really integrated traditional stepping into your body, move on to more complex drunken methods. Never let go of your foundations. At the very least, going back to your basic stepping and movement patterns makes for a solid warmup pattern. Speaking of which, it's never a bad idea to start with this:

INSTEP JUMPS: From a low *mabu*, jump as high as you can. As you jump, the soles of your feet touch together, thus creating an arc with your feet / legs. It's like clapping the soles of your feet together. If seen from the front, each foot traces the shape of a circle in opposing directions. Landing on the ground again in another deep *mabu* should be silent, dissipating the impact into the springiness of the legs and body's natural shock absorbing abilities. Try for increasing your height range over time.

DAILY DOSE: Ten of these before your workout should provide a good warmup / cooldown for any leg workout. Add more repetitions as required.

FOUNDATIONAL BOXING STEPS

For all of these, keep your hands up. Even better, keep them *alive*, moving, and integrated into the drills. Unintentionally sloppy hands will see you taking many hits on the chin.

DIRECTIONAL SLIDING STEPS: From a basic fighting stance, whichever direction you need to move in, that foot moves first, doing so with as little "hop" as possible to avoid head movement bobbing up and down. Aim for horizontal shifting rather than and up-down jump. For instance, from a left leg forward stance, if you need to move forward, the left foot moves forward first, and the right foot follows suit. Moving backwards is reversed. Moving left; left leg moves first. Moving right; right leg moves first.

DAILY DOSE: In your practice space, do sets of ten.
-Ten forward, ten backward, ten left, ten right.
-Ten clockwise (forward, R, back, L), then ten counterclockwise (forward, L, back, R) square patterns.
-Ten diagonal forward and backward.

Change sides, repeat.

SHUFFLE STEPS: As above, but this time the rear leg moves first. In other words, if you're moving forward, the rear leg slides into position, and the front leg then moves forward into place. Reverse this for backwards movement. Moving right; left leg moves first. Moving left; right leg moves first.

DAILY DOSE: In your practice space, do sets of ten.

-Ten forward, ten backward, ten left, ten right.
-Ten clockwise (forward, R, back, L), then ten counterclockwise (forward, L, back, R) square patterns.
-Ten diagonal forward and backward.

Change sides, repeat.

PIVOT: As though there is a long metal spike driven through your foot, protruding from the *yongquan* point in the center of the sole and pinning you to the earth: this is how you'll pivot on the leading leg, spinning backwards. So, if your left leg is forward, you'll pivot clockwise on your left sole, 180 degrees. Various hand methods coordinate with this, the simplest is to land a left hook, finishing all movement right as the pivot ends. Avoid height changes and off-kilter swivels as much as possible (for now), and strive for speed.

DAILY DOSE: Sets of ten. Both sides. Several sets to warm up.

STEP, PIVOT: As above, but this time you step first, then pivot. As an example: left foot forward, I step forward so my right foot is leading, and quickly pivot on my right foot, 180 counter-clockwise.

DAILY DOSE: Sets of ten. Several sets to warm up.

MIX IT UP: Create various combinations of all of the above stepping patterns, keeping your hands alive throughout, even shadowboxing as you do so. Be sure to do forward, backward, diagonal, and different repetitions of each. Examples are Shuffle x 2, Pivot (on either front or rear foot). Slide x 2, Pivot. Slide, Shuffle, Pivot-step-pivot.

DAILY DOSE: Create one set, then repeat it ten times each side. Continue until it's second nature.

STEPS OF THE LOTUS / LOTUS STEPPING

One of the beautiful things about the drunken lotus stepping, is that it embodies the entire core stepping methods from *zui quan*. The fact that it also looks relatively simple is a hint towards how the entire system is predicated on deceptive projections. Once the gross coordination is understood, the transitions between postures should really be explored. The spectrum of "drunkenness" and "sloppiness" should also be examined, never actually losing control, while appearing to do so. Broken down into rigid "snapshots" of its core movements, it contains all of the classic traditional *gong fu* stances: horse, bow, empty, X, nail, leaning. Analyzed for its motion, it's all arcs and sweeping circularity, which can be interjected with linear leg skills if needed. Footwork also is done with various intricacies and weight adjustments. Other considerations are: each step is an attack, each attack is a step through, multiple sweeping methods are available, *dantian* drives sloshing and whipping. Mechanically, there is the loosening of the major joints – hips, knees, ankles, shoulders, elbows, wrists. Meditatively, explore the rhythms and breaking them, and study how *dantian* disseminates force around and throughout the entire body, all the while letting the form move you, and observe how breath overlays with the physical movements.

INSTRUCTION

This is for moving counter-clockwise, and is reversed for clockwise stepping. Begin in a left-leading bow stance. The right leg cross steps forward at a 45-degree angle into an X-stance. The left (now rear) leg moves directly left until you're standing in a right-leading bow stance. Draw the right leg back to a right-leading empty stance (majority of weight on left leg), then to a nail stance. The (now weightless) right foot steps directly right into a left-leaning stance. Move the weight to the center into a low horse stance. Shift weight onto the right leg as you draw the left leg to a left nail stance. Step forward to a right empty stance, weight is still on the right leg. Continue sliding it forward until you're in a left-leading bow stance, at which point you're back to the starting position. Repeat. This is the stepping pattern if broken down into its rigid minutiae. When you actually start doing the stepping with fluidity, it's more akin to (1) Left bow stance, cross step to (2) Right leg forward X stance, to (3) Right bow stance, to (4) horse stance, to (5) Left bow stance (6) Repeat. Grossly simplified, but these are the broad strokes.

The *Steps of the Lotus* repeat multiple times throughout the form, and are even considered one of the fundamental practices of *zui quan*. Within old systems of Chinese fighting arts, motions with this type of repetitive appearance in a form very clearly indicate vital skills to examine and integrate. Unfortunately, the showmanship of the stumbling steps are often mistaken for just that: *theatrics*, so their true application and utility are commonly overlooked. Along with all of the stepping, footwork, weight transfers, and attacks within the pattern, keep in mind the concepts of structure, strong disguised as weak appearance, and power connection to your core. Continuous flow is vital, and even the term 蓮花 ("lotus flower"), is used as a play on the word "continuous". Also referred to as 醉酒似退實進 ("drunk appears to retreat, actually advances"), this name explicitly states the deceptive elements contained within the pattern.

Depending on your level or focus for the day, there are different ways to approach the stumbling steps. Some suggestions are outlined below, but you will naturally find your own as you progress. In order to make the most of a training session, it's a good idea to choose one tiny aspect of this enormously valuable movement pattern, and work on just that element for the session.

FLAGS: No flow: using the various stances contained within to pause at static points ("flag points"), effectively training a stance-shifting drill. Keep stances as low as possible, not technically stopping at the flag points, but transitioning slowly.

HONEY: Slow, heavy, methodical transitions from piece to piece, as though you were immersed in a thick, viscous liquid like honey. All steps downward are slow and deliberate; no "dropping" or breaking pace allowed.

WHIPPING: All kicks and motions are driven from *dantian* in a whipping energy, which necessitates dealing with the recoil of such movement. Naturally, start slow to avoid injury, dialing power up as you go.

SLOSHING: Similar to above, but keeping a sloshing energy throughout, playing around with the conservation of energy created as the "wine" sloshing around inside generates more energy and power.

SPEED: Done as quick as possible, without letting all the mechanical components derail. In other words, it shouldn't be a random, speedy mess at the expense of proper technique. If it does get too messy, dial it back, then repeat.

SLOW & LIGHT: Pace is as slow as possible, but delicately; if you move to quickly, you'll break. If you step too harshly, you'll break things around you. As such, you move slowly and meditatively, feeling the air pressure resist your motion.

KICKS: Every single motion is a kick.

ATTACKS: Every single motion is an attack (different from above: consider all parts of your anatomy).

SWEEPS: Every single motion is a sweep.

BLOCKS: Every single motion is a block, check, or deflection.

MINDSETS of the Drunkard: An "angry" drunkard is going to move with more fiery rage and fierceness than a "playful" drunk, who is going to naturally move differently than a "hungover" or "blacked out" drunk. "Male" and "female" dichotomies will also express drunkenness distinctly, not to mention the "sickly" embodiment.

HANDS / ARMS: play around with your arms: letting them hang loose at your sides to explore how your core moves them with various degrees of relaxation employed. Keep hands and arms held in a "barrel" posture in front, arms essentially held in a structure with the majority of motion in the legs. "Tending the bar" or "Wiping the table" motions and spirals with the hands as you train the set. Shadow boxing with basic strikes. Long Fist arm swings.

Arms extended at shoulder-height out the sides, thus creating a very

clear feedback loop as to how the body / arms react to the *dantian-*

driven legs.

DAILY DOSE:

This should be the lion's share of your practice once you go down
the drunken path.

-Ten forward, ten reverse.
-Choose ONE of the above methods and practice it until it's second-
nature.
-Try doing the stepping pattern as you locomote around the training
space, which necessitates altering the stepping sizes and mechanics.
Use it as a means to cover distance.

Change sides, repeat.

ADVANCED PRACTICE

Once you've advanced further with the lotus steps, they can be

integrated with other elements of training. One of my teachers had us

imagine a *bagua* diagram on the floor, over which we'd use the lotus

steps to move around sequentially to the various *guas*. Movement

from one space to another uses a variety of different stepping or

stumbling. Each trigram requires doing a smaller, compact rendition of the lotus stepping, ensuring that it is done multiple times while

traversing around the room / the circle.

In the diagram below, each depiction of the lotus flower is a space where one would do a smaller version of the lotus stepping before moving onwards to another *gua*. It also shows one advanced training paradigm, described below:

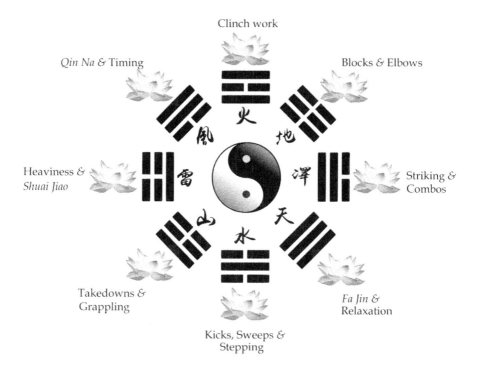

After this becomes natural in both directions, the next element is to

incorporate different training components to each *gua*. As one moves

around the circle and arrives at a certain trigram, a distinct training

module is used while occupying that space (see above for one such

regimen). If you maintain this as strictly a footwork drill, the above-

described focuses would be done using the legs only, for example.

How legs are used for "kicking" should be patently obvious, but perhaps less so with something like "*Qin Na*" or "Grappling". While the actual techniques may vary depending upon the current training focus and requirements, the structure of the drill is clear. It should also be made abundantly clear that this type of training is reserved for advanced practitioners, as there is a massive volume of mental focus and many distinct capabilities running concurrently when done correctly. Its methodology also overlaps with the breakdown of the Eight Immortals archetypes outlined later in this book, which has training structured in a similar way.

"Stepping follows changes of the body."

THE OLD BAG
Exploring the "Boxing" of Drunken Boxing

by Wang Kunshan

Finding in-depth analysis and viable examples of drunken boxing sparring techniques is indeed a rarity, and often leads to finding schools that simply practice one or two *zui quan tao lu* (drunken fist forms) rather than actually engaging in drunken combat. At the end of the day, true combative skills require methodical repetition of relevant techniques and shadow boxing, included in tandem with pressure testing with resisting opponents who can push the envelope and help to hone your methods.

Like any other Chinese based martial arts, authentic drunken fist expresses in a well-rounded curriculum of health benefiting drills (*qigong*, *neigong*, yogic stretching, cardiovascular stimulation), mindful cultivation (meditation, *neigong*, mindset archetypes), and of course combative skills (self-defense, boxing, striking, takedowns, *qin na*, grappling, submissions). While still a relatively rare and misunderstood martial art, it has grown in popularity in more recent years, with both positive and negative results. On one hand, its proliferation has led to more student numbers and the requisite scrutiny that goes along with such a phenomenon. On the other hand, with an increased student pool also comes the dilution of the training methods, and often incorrect transmissions of the principles, tactics and skills inherent in traditional *zui quan gong fu*. Put simply, the *gong fu* often falls victim to the double-edged sword of popularizing an art. That having been said, there still exist a number of practitioners who strive to maintain the "martial" aspect of the training, and who subscribe to the fundamental principles of a solid and practical fighting method. Dances are pretty; fighting is practical.

Frequent and practical sparring is a necessary tenet of *Zui Quan* practice. The forms, like in any Chinese gong fu, do not directly impart fighting ability. Simple. It's only by putting miles on the fighting path that one can correctly cultivate speed, distance, timing, angles, balance-imbalance, and stamina. You get good at what you train, so the question to ask is what exactly are you training?

"Excuses are easy; seeking out training opportunities is harder."

PRICIER TOYS

Not always available, affordable, or practical for some practitioners and training spaces, it should be noted that "where there's a will, there's a way". Training partners, acquaintances, local fitness facilities, or gyms may have some of the following equipment, and making the opportunities arise to use them shouldn't be passed up. Excuses are easy; seeking out training opportunities is harder.

HEAVY BAG: Heavy bag practice is a "must" for training, for several reasons. The weight of a heavy bag mimics the dynamic of a real opponent in that it absorbs the impacts of strikes in a similar way to how an adversary's body would. This allows you to explore using a varied spectrum of power in your strikes while receiving immediate feedback on how you land your hits. In other words, you can feel what it's like to express full power in your attacks and see how it feels in terms of structural integrity in your own body, as well as feel how much resistance a solid target offers. You quickly get a real sense of any gaps or disconnects in your entire system. Any imperfections in skill or structure are seen as discomfort or even injury as you increase power, repetitions, or both. This type of full-force repetitive training is a simple-yet-effective feedback system for making micro or macro adjustments in real time. It goes without saying that developing striking power and full body connection through said strikes is important.

Another benefit to working on a heavy bag is that it allows you to explore targeting and work on target accuracy in terms of relative positioning to one's own body. You can judge targets on an opponent in based on where they are in relation to your own anatomy. Let's take a left hook as a simple illustration of this idea. While stationary, you can visualize exactly how high a target is when you position your body alignments and make impact, using your own body as a metric for determining the placement of the hit. While seemingly obvious, it's regularly taken for granted how our minds process and adapt to heights, distances and angles presented in order to make a correct and effective strike. Your left hook should make contact with the target at the appropriate height and angle, and your own joints should not be compromised. A common error is to make adjustments which adversely affect one's own structure when adapting to a larger or smaller opponent or striking surface. Put simply: use your own body to judge where to hit on the heavy bag, and do it with correct body alignments. This gets even trickier when you're putting yourself into the unusual positions and calibrations of drunken fist.

One further benefit is that it necessitates footwork while training various strikes, including body, elbow, and shoulder strikes. As the bag freely swings around, you need to use your stepping to adjust range and positioning, and it happily takes full power hits and kicks. It's great for playing around with drunken lotus stepping, stumbling, or movements like *"Drunken Han Dances on Clouds"*. It readily becomes apparent when the flow between your upper and lower components is lacking.

While a great part of one's arsenal, this training tool has some limitations to keep in mind. The swaying and movement of the weighted mass becomes quickly predictable, making it an easy target to hit. On top of this, it doesn't give much to react to in terms of "hitting back", so it can lead to complacency with keeping awareness and your guards up. Overall, it's a pretty fun inclusion in the training.

SPEED BAG: It's used for imparting identification of timing and rhythm, building endurance, and helping to develop quick, dangerous hands. Agility built up from being able to keep the bag going for a good period of time is the type that helps you jab and strike through an opponent's defenses. Oftentimes,  people assume drunken fist fighters are slow and lumbering, so having the capacity for high velocity, rapid-fire strikes is an important part of the deceptive aspect to this *quan*.

The repetitive nature of this device makes it quickly apparent how it conditions the shoulder and arm muscles, as well as increases stamina, which is always an asset. Relaxed fluidity eventually is established as over-tension results in exhaustion: nervous tension has to give way to proper technique. On top of this, a speed bag's rapid movement helps fine-tune accuracy and hand-eye coordination, and can "hit back", meaning that it can hand out slightly painful reminders to keep your guard and awareness up.

Additionally, this tool can help sort out imbalances between left and right sides in terms of speed, accuracy, and coordination. Reaction time on both sides should get smoothed-out over time, too. With regular use of the speed bag, these discrepancies start to even-out if you're mindfully and symmetrically training.

The downside to this tool is that it doesn't generally require full body movements and stepping to ensure accurate strikes. In other words, it's very "hand-focused". Its predictability can also lead to mindless punching sessions, but even this can peripherally result in some of the positive benefits described above. One other limiting factor to this device is that it's quite noisy, so you won't be making friends with your neighbors with early morning workouts. While relatively cheap to buy, they're rarely seen outside of boxing gyms for this reason.

DOUBLE-END BAG: Some say this device is the unique child of a heavy bag and a speed bag, in that it has some of the benefits of both, combined in its own special package. Like a speed bag, it requires accurate and rhythmic strikes, and like a heavy bag, it can take hard-hitting punishment, and requires footwork and movement to use. It's a tiny, moving target, so it requires the type of accuracy found in honed hand-eye coordination and hours spent relaxing into proper timing. Unlike the cumbersome, solid heavy bag, the double-end bag necessitates accuracy and quick reflexes to hit with effective strikes. It can be framed this way: your opponent's darting motions are going to be more akin to a double-end bag than a heavy bag.

Rhythm is a key part of high-level *gong fu*, and like anything, needs to be honed in stages. Constant movement of the double-end bag necessitates understanding patterns of motion and triggers comprehension of when to actually throw strikes. Strong rhythm makes a drunken fighter formidable. Somewhat mimicking an opponent's bobbing and weaving head, squarely hitting the bag as it darts back and forth is a functional challenge for this training.

CHEAPER TOYS

LET'S FIGHT

When starting out, the sparring is done at a slow, relaxed, almost meditative pace. One must become accustomed to the irregularities of the positions while under the pressure dynamic of facing off against an opponent who could potentially want to "ring your bell". Form training is what imparts the shapes one must adhere to for the style, but adapting them correctly to fighting is something that needs to be ramped up to, and done so with a methodical approach. Counter-intuitively, it's this slow approach which leads to correct physical power being expressed through the drunken style.

The challenge to overcome in the initial stages is reverting back to one's comfort zone and utilizing prevailing methods. Naturally, one must have a strong foundation in traditional *sanda* / *quanfa* methods, which should have given the experience of being in a competitive combat sport scenario. The adrenaline, stresses, and mindset of being in a ring or on a *leitai* should not be foreign to a fighter.

The initial approach of a slow, controlled pace is essential to achieve true balance, coordination, structures, *fang song* (tension-relaxation balance), and breathing. This teaches you to move easily, freely, and without undue tension so that you can muster proper structural integrity behind your martial drunken movements, and not just "look" drunken and wobbly. There absolutely needs to be "method" to your drunken madness.

Some teachers even break up boxing training into three distinct phases, which in turn can be overlaid with three tempos. Phase one involves correction of postures, structures and geometries (which should be imbedded within the forms of the style). Phase two involves applications and patterns (which are transposed to self-defense scenarios as well). Phase three has to do with conditioning, but specifically with coordination of breathing techniques into motions. Further levels of training exist, but these three set the stage for drunken boxing foundations.

The tempos referred to include 1. complete relaxation and slow pace, 2. mid-level speed but no power, and finally, 3. high intensity speed that focusses on entire body recruitment. Naturally, the paces need to be worked on and internalized in this sequence.

It may be surprising to note how common it is to lack the ability to coordinate hands and feet. This is the phase of POSTURE that must have adequate time devoted to it. Focus should be on the expression of the static SHAPES of the form as they're put in motion and transition from one to the next in a proper manner. Some teachers posit that through mastery of posture, one can truly acquire and express proper, flexible strength. One must be careful of misunderstanding such simplifications. Arriving at this level is usually quite rare, as the desire to progress often results in students sabotaging their own skills by jumping forward- before they're actually ready to move on.

DAILY DOSE

Find where you fit in to the three phases described above, and tailor your training accordingly. Devote enough time to mastery of each.

Train the different tempos discussed above, and be able to switch between them at will.

Invest in some 12 or 14 oz gloves and hand wraps, as the number of repetitions required will not be kind to your hands at full force. STRETCH and warmup before any punching bag workout. Don't learn this the hard way. Work conventional jabs, crosses, hooks, uppercuts, starting slow and with low power to ensure you're achieving proper bone alignment and striking surfaces. Have prescribed routine, something measurable and quantifiable. For example, do 6, 3-minute rounds, with a 1-minute break in between, set to a timer. Start relatively stationary while you warm up, before integrating body movement and stepping as part of your shadow boxing. Start with hands only, then do legs only (then elbows, knees, body), before integrating both / all. Explore power dynamics, such as doing 5 light strikes, followed by 3 full-power ones. Work prescribed combinations that are part of your repertoire before ever doing any sort of "freestyle" or very drunken training. Also, always do a cool down after a session, moving and lightly striking the bag, moving your feet, and calming your respiration.

Other round options: Hands only. Legs only. Left or Right side strikes only. Only jabs (or crosses, etc.) but constantly change heights. Light strikes to heavy (described above), or vice versa.

Become familiar with, and adept at, standard gym and boxing equipment, so that you can adapt it to your drunken needs and progress.

Sparring partners, especially for *zui quan*, are not always easy to come by, so using conventional gear as a proxy can still yield positive results. That said, take advantage of having an able and willing partner when you can. Make sure you have goals and parameters laid out for both of you in order to make the most of this time together. Plan what to work on, and drill it properly so it settles into your body, and becomes fine wine.

LASHING OUT AND HITTING THINGS
Exploring the "Boxing Combos" of Drunken Boxing

by Ma Hao Xing

One of the key components to this training is being on the receiving end. In this case, that means holding onto practice pads as your training partner uses various ranges of power, all the way up to full. There is much to be learned from holding the pads correctly. Given that drunken boxing is considered a high-level art, it's important to have a strong foundational grasp of Orthodox methods, which includes pad holding. It's been said: How can you bend and break the rules if you don't know what they are? For instance, when holding the pads, you have to know which angle to hold them at to avoid injury and impart efficacy to your training partner. You also have to know how to meet the incoming strike with the appropriate force dynamic. Unfortunately, there are many so-called "fighters" out there who have never been hit, and therefore have no real idea what they'd be in for during an actual altercation. This is not meant as some sort of "tough guy" ethos, rather, it's a solution to the fairy-tale thinking that pervades too many traditional arts. Striking and holding pads is in itself a very visceral form of training body methods. In fact, there should be full body connection, concentration, and awareness while meeting a strike.

So, what does this have to do with drunken fist? Knowing how conventional strikes work is important for knowing your conventional opponents. You should study how these strikes work, and pay attention to your reactions, especially when they get up to high speeds and more power. Very pragmatic things to study include: What angles do they come in at? At what point of impact do they have more power? What are their targets? Pad holding should not be a mindless routine of standing and getting bashed around.

When actually doling out these strikes, you should pay attention to your full body connection and how you are deriving and driving force from the ground. As you strike, study your own reactions within. As with holding pads, you should remain mindful, and not mentally wander off into patterns and rhythms of just pounding away on your partner. With these straightforward methods, it should be easy to notice when your structure is misaligned or your power is compromised.

With all of this in mind, you should be able to overlay it with your drunken training to know when that is lacking as well. Essentially, you should use it as a template for power, angles, and alignment reference. When you get into the unusual positions of drunken boxing you should be able to express the same amounts of power, angling, and force, but it should look far different – in terms of shapes, stances, and attacking methods. This creates a baseline for your training. Without establishing a baseline for your own abilities, you won't have a true cognizance of what it means to push those limits. This includes measurable phenomena, such as stamina, power, spirals, alignment, force, and technique.

Having a familiarity with mainstream combinations also makes it easier to find training partners when you just need to get in a workout. It's far more common to find somebody who is able to do orthodox pad holding and give you a good cardio workout than to find a drunken master to stray into unconventional *gong fu* training. Despite what some internal martial artists may tell you, physical conditioning is extremely important.

TRAINING PARTNERS

Being a good training partner is a vital skill, and there is so much to learn from being on the receiving end of things. Shutting down a technique that you know is coming is pretty much useless. Let your partner complete the techniques, and study things such as impact, imbalance, locks, strangulation, etc. In this way, you'll also feel the various stages of a technique being carried out, which is invaluable information. For instance, if you always escape early from a *qin na* lock, you'll never know the spectrum of feelings such an attack creates, and therefore won't have escapes for these situations if you ever mess up and they play out. "Invest in loss" is one way of explaining this. All of this is necessary for striking and pad holding practice as well.

DAILY DOSE

So, after all this discourse and theory, what should you actually be practicing? The repetitions, intensity and duration of your training depends on your level, but the actual combinations can be trained by all. These all assume you have a foundational understanding of throwing a proper jab (1), cross (2), lead hook (3), rear hook (4), lead uppercut (5) and rear uppercut (6). Not only should you be able to respond to the numbers called, you should be able to call out combos. Here are some useful pattern sets to integrate into your practice:

A. 1, 2, 5, 2

B. 1, 6, 3, 2

C. 6, 3, 3

D. 1, 2, 3 high, 3 low

E. 1, 3 low, 3 low, 3 high

F. 1, Slip a Jab, 1, 2, 1

G. 1, 2, Slip a Jab, 4 (low or high)

H. 2, 3, Slip Jab, Low 3

Once you're warmed up and have these dialed in, you should include these, which have a more "interactive" element to them:

I. 1, 2, 3, 2, Bob a L hook, 2, 3, 2, Bob a R hook, 3, 2, 3

J. 1, 2, Slip a Jab, 2, 3, Slip a Cross, 3, 2, 3

K. 1, 2, 3, Slip a Cross, 3 to low body, 3 to head, 2

You'll notice that these don't include kicks, knees, or elbows, which is intentional. Isolate and sort out the segments before combining them into a whole, or the entire system suffers.

MOMENTUM

Achieving proper mechanics during combinations is actually a vital component of *conservation of momentum*, which is actually a big part of correct combat arts, including drunken boxing. For instance, throw a basic jab, and as you retract it, you use that energy of the retraction to correctly pivot and throw your cross. Throwing a powerful cross, followed immediately by another one with the same limb not only feels awkward, it requires far more energy expenditure. Doing it properly is a very gross and obvious manifestation of this "conservation of momentum". Once your body is put into motion, you economize your subsequent movements through intelligent reactions: as one limb is retracted, it creates the situation of correct physics for sending out the opposite one.

While in some of the given combinations you strike twice with the same limb (such as, the double lead hooks, above), the momentum is conserved and calibrated via body movement, bouncing, or elliptical motion. If done properly, it does not violate the principles discussed; rather, it highlights them — if done correctly.

This is found in many athletic and combat endeavors. The skills contained within drunken boxing are not new or magical, they are simply hiding or exaggerating these types of conservation of momentum. The movements are either largely comical and exaggerated, or diminished and hidden so as not to be apparent. High skill is being able to appropriately express the most effective one.

Conventional boxers are skilled fighters because they take a very small and defined set of skills, then pressure-test them *ad nauseam* until they fill in any gaps. This is great, and is also something which should be a part of a good *gong fu* fighter's arsenal. If you have a strong command of these established methods of fighting, you should be able to analyze and dissect them, and express them either in a larger fashion or in a more subtle way. This is drunken fist.

RAGDOLL DRILL

This is the description of a drill from *The Path of Drunken Boxing* book by Zhang Jing Fa. A simple, yet solid drill to work on for the basis of movement conservation is sometimes called the "ragdoll drill".

Standing with your eyes closed, completely relax, releasing as much as possible throughout your structure. Your training partner is tasked with pushing on various parts of your body—not enough to imbalance and knock you over, but enough to cause obvious shifting of your frame. Your feet remain planted in place, meaning that there is to be no stepping for this specific drill. As the recipient of the force, you must feel and react to the incoming pushes by having it express elsewhere. Basically, this is a method for calibrating deficiency and excess: *yin* and *yang*. Absorbing is *yin*, while outward projection is *yang*. Your entire body and limbs remain relaxed, loose, and heavy, using your awareness to do mental "sweeps" throughout your own anatomy as the exercise is happening. Remain acutely aware of where you're absorbing force and therefore *yin*, and contrast this with the created *yang* that arises by another part of your body that adjusts to maintain equilibrium. Boil it all down to two simple questions: Where am I *yin*? Where am I *yang*? This deficiency / excess dichotomy is a three-dimensional phenomenon, so your awareness needs to be integrated with your body: how it's moving, being moved, and reacting.

From the book *The Path of Drunken Boxing*:

"Your partner should start facing you, and push on either shoulder or either hip. They can also pull on these areas to practice the same effect. For example, if my partner uses his right hand to push my left shoulder back, my right shoulder is naturally going to come forward so I can maintain my balance. As you become more proficient, your partner can add more force, press on different areas, or combine different "attacks", all with the goal of affecting you in three dimensions of motion. Pay specific attention to your three dan tians: how they move independently and in relation to each other during these drills. You can isolate movement to a one or two dan tians in order to work specific motions or skills, but always be aware of your actions.

There is a lot to be taken from this drill, so it should be done as often as possible. Skills can develop in balance, sensitivity, movement in multiple planes, defense/attack formulation, and overall body awareness. Both *yin* and *yang* polarities of this drill can be used for both attack and defense. *Yin* can absorb or evade defensively, or "disappear" structurally to lead into throws or sweeps. *Yang* movements can manifest offensively in strikes, elbows or *kao* (heavy body) attacks, and be utilized defensively in parries or evasions. Because of the fluctuating nature of *yin-yang*, there are usually elements of both, especially in more established drunken players."

SHAKING YOUR POLE

Pole Shaking Training

by Shifu Neil Ripski

Pole Shaking is one of those often referred to and rarely explained publicly training exercises that seem to carry a sense of the esoteric with it. There are various methods of pole shaking found in many different arts and all of them are working towards the same goal of connectivity, structure, power and the ability to emit force over a distance. That in itself sounds pretty far out but that distance is not referring to projecting *qi* through the air it is getting the power generated within the body to the hands or ideally through the extension of the body, the pole, in order to carry it into an opponent's body in combat.

One of the things mentioned about the exercise is that it trains the 丹田 (*Dantian*). Unfortunately, often times this is left as a statement that students just accept and are left wondering what that means and to hope something good will happen over time. If the exercises are trained and corrected, well then, yes, the *Dantian* will be trained and power will be generated but what does that actually mean?

Dantian is not just a space under the navel where "*qi*" is stored, it is that from a certain point of view but it is also not just that as well. Using the word *Dantian* is referring to many things and like any Chinese concept needs context for any discussion. Briefly the idea that it, "stores post-heaven *qi* that is used to perform the functions of daily life," means that the things you put in it like food, water, and so on, give one a good feeling in that area, thereby allow you to have energy that you can then use for your life. It is "post-heaven" (*hou tian*) because it is gathered after you are born.

Martial artists refer to *Dantian* as a place where movement originates in the body, and since it is the center of mass and the location of many different muscle groups in the abdomen (Psoas, Iliacus, upper and lower abdominals, etc.), it is a powerful place where muscular chains of movement can be activated and radiate outwards through the body. The ability to move those muscles first in the torso, and have that twisting (捻勁, niǎn jìn) power cascade upwards and downwards through the torso to the limbs, allows more and more muscle groups to be added to the force of the movement. In this way, by the time a movement ripples out to the hand, many various groups of muscle have activated to continue to accelerate and generate force for when that hand touches an opponent.

Pole shaking then requires the *Dantian* to be moved first in order to create the cascade of muscular contraction throughout the body needed in order to move a heavy stick with enough force to shake it at the completion of movement. In order to do this *Dantian* must be "tightened like the head of a drum," meaning an engagement of the abdomen that is not "tightening" nor "relaxed" or "loose". The head of a drum must be tuned by stretching it to create a desired tone. The abdomen needs to be engaged in a way that creates tonus in the muscle beyond its natural state, but still having much more ability to engage. If I were to arbitrarily put percentages to it, then I would say the *Dantian* should be 10 – 20% engaged before movement begins, in order to create connectivity through the torso, especially for cross body engagement. Pole shaking is like weight lifting for the *Dantian*.

A good pole for the training will be heavy enough that the player needs to engage the *Dantian* in order to effectively move it without relying on the arms alone. If it is too light, it is easy to cheat and try to shake it with the arms only. However, it should not be so heavy as to be unwieldy for a person to lift. In my experience a pole of *Bai La Mu* (白蠟木, White Wax Wood) is not only the traditional material for the pole, but is a perfect material for flex. You can pole shake with a hardwood staff but it simply won't shake, so it will be hard to get the feedback to know if you are doing it well. Furthermore, when you generate enough force to try and shake a pole, any mistakes in your own structure can cause you harm. Something is going to shake: either you or the pole, simple as that. When I first started learning it, I was told it was not safe to shake a hardwood pole. Being me, I tried anyway when Shifu was not around, and dislocated a vertebra in my neck.... Get a soft flexible pole. I would caution against rattan, simply because it is too flexible and easy to shake; you don't want easy, you want training.

So long as the movements of the pole shaking are done with *Dantian* moving first, the *Dantian* engaged, and the rest of the body engaging towards its extremities throughout the movement, then over time, as everything gets more coordinated and you become stronger all over, the pole will start to shake. Each movement of the pole should have a shaking quality to it when you pause. The typical variant is 攔 (*Lan*: Obstruct), 拿 (*Na*: Sieze), 扎 (*Zha*: Stab) from Chinese spear training, and each movement should have the shake from the power emitting from the body. It's not as easy as it sounds.

To train one side is to limit your progress and understanding. In this case, the physical movements and engagements of the *Dantian* and rest of the body are the *Yang* 陽 – the tissue, the thing you can touch like the earth, the physical. The *Yin* 陰 aspect – the untouchable, the ethereal like the moon or heaven is the mind. Once the physical movements are trained and become fairly natural, one generally finds that the pole does not want to shake yet or does not move very much, especially in comparison to more advanced players. A caution about using a pole that is extremely long and flexible: it is very easy to shake such a stick, and that gives one a false sense of accomplishment. If it is too easy, it is not training; if it is too hard, it is not useful. Balance, as always, is the key.

The mind must be free from the basic movements in order to train the more *Yin* (ethereal) side of the exercise. Once the mind is no longer concentrating on the basic fundamentals of the movements- - like shoulders down, scapula pulled towards the waist, neck long like listening behind you, *Dantian* tightened like the head of a drum, pressing the earth away from you with the feet, standing *in* your legs not *on* them, spine straight from 大椎 (*Da Zhui*) to 命門 (*Mingmen*), elbows closer to the body than your wrists, knees remaining above the feet through each movement, and so on-- then the mind can be freed to work on the intention that creates the long power (*Chang Jin* 長勁), which is the specialty of the spear and pole shaking practices.

Chang Jin means power that can travel a long way. This does not mean traversing through the air to hit opponents like video game-style fireballs, it means power that can travel through the body or weapon you hold, and then transfer into an opponent. Ideally, this is either right through them to cause internal damage, or to throw them away. The mind during the pole shaking exercises simply needs to be "reaching" through the pole past its extreme end. It is like reaching for your keys under the couch and trying to make your arm just a few inches longer. In bare-handed training I tell students to reach through their fingers in the same way. This allows connectivity and power to reach your fingertips. Training with a long pole and doing this same mental training allows for the pole to become more a part of your body, rather than just something you are holding, and that connection allows the power you generate to more easily reach the pole's tip. Mental change creates physical change, in the same way our posture changes when we experience emotions like grief or joy. Changing how we think as we move changes what happens within us as we move. This is one of the many reasons martial artists benefit from meditative practices to strengthen the mind. Without a focused mind, free from distractions this type, progress is very hard to achieve.

Pole shaking was a huge turning point for me in my training; nothing ever gave me a more visceral feeling of connection in so little time. It was one of the few exercises I was made to do and trust, and saw results quickly in both technique practice and sparring, with and without weapons. I could not recommend it more.

INVISIBLE DISTANCE: BE MIST

EXPAND & COMPRESS

Drunken Kicking & Striking

by Ma Hao Xing

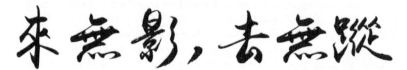

"Come and go without a trace." – 西遊記 / *Journey to the West*

Drunken boxing performances across styles, despite some superficial differences, tend to have various technique and skills that overlap, especially when it comes to core concepts and theories. Many times, the underlying importance of a movement has been lost when practitioners gravitate towards performative *wushu*, film, or demonstration situations, so it's important to recognize the difference between these and actual combative applicability. A term very commonly bandied about with drunken boxing is "deception", which definitely needs to be part of a *zui quan* player's arsenal. However, it's silly to think that an opponent will suddenly be tricked into believing you're actually drunk, when just moments before you were sober. If your adversary is so easily deceived, you're lucky, as there won't be much of a fight ahead of you.

Instead, the idea of "deceiving" someone takes on far more nuance, which only really comes from years of devoted study, application, and pressure testing. With that in mind, we can explore this concept using a very common example that is found in many drunken forms. While not alone in its integration of this skill, drunken style *gong fu* uses a lot of "invisible distance". A very base level example of this is the extra range one can achieve by turning the body slightly. For instance, if you stand with your back to a wall and punch straight in front with your right fist while keeping your shoulders parallel to said wall, your punching range is only as far as your arm is long. However, if you retract your left shoulder as you turn your spine and extend your right shoulder forward, your range increases much more as you turn. This simplified version of achieving additional range is what we'll call "invisible distance", and is found in many arts.

Expressed in the idea of Compressing and Expanding (sometimes also referred to as "Closing" and "Opening"), we'll reference this later to illustrate training methods that are relevant. Simply stated, **Compressing** is making one's body smaller in order to appear further away, weak, or unseen, while **Expanding** is taking up more space, appearing larger, attacking or extending. The staccato nature of many drunken forms is a way to represent or conceal this type of technique. Many "drinks" are like this, and have a staggered nature or faltering appearance. This is a big part of the "Broken Timing" of drunkard's style boxing, which refers to executing attacks and movements with differing speeds, changing tempos, or unexpected pacing to make them harder to deal with. This concept becomes layered with the potential of multi-directional movements, thereby making attacks much more unpredictable, and much harder to anticipate and negate.

Packaging these together – *Compressing, Expanding, Broken Timing, Multi-directional Motion* – we end up with core components of the "deception" of drunken fist. In fact, one drunken boxing teacher said that the goal of being an effective *zui quan* combatant is to be continually imperceptible – "***be like mist***".

So, how does one begin the training of this ideation? First, it's about exploring the duality of Compression & Expansion using known techniques. Because line training is a great way to ensure repetition of techniques on both sides, we'll begin with basic kicks. As first trained, there is no "drunken" engine running the motions, which would include things like "sloshing" to drive heaviness into the kick, target changes, or broken timing. Rather, the initial focus is simply on Compression & Expansion.

METHOD

A basic standard front kick from a left-leading *gong bu* stance has the person draw up to right-leg-up crane stance, extend the right kick, withdraw to crane, then step back, repeating kicks again and again with the same (right) leg. Our drunken variation begins with this foundation.

1. From a left-leading *gong bu* stance facing south, 2. draw up to a right-leg-up crane stance (compress), 3. extend the kick to the south (expand), but don't retract it back to crane. 4. Instead, quickly and smoothly pivot on the ball of your left foot so your hips face east, as your kick becomes a side kick to the south (expand), all done in one swift "pop" motion without retracting it. The pivoting on the foot and swivel of the hips gives extra range and distance. Both of these kicks should have power to them, although the second one will have noticeably less when starting out. As you begin to play around with timings and distances, there can be various stages of retraction that are utilized, which will also affect the power of the kick. 5. After the side kick, quickly pivot on the left foot again as you retract the kick

into a right-leg-up crane stance facing south again (compress). Very simply, this sequence demonstrates: 2. Compression > 3. Expansion > 4. Expansion > 5. Compression.

1.   2.   3.

4.   5.   6.

6. Step forward with the right leg so you're now in a right-leading *gong bu*, and repeat on the other side, walking forward (and then later, backwards as well) in a line. These are not necessarily intended as "fight ending" strikes, but instead are ways to chip away at the opponent's physical and mental defenses (deceptively). Effectively, you're training a combination of Compress (crane), Expand (front kick), Expand further (side kick), Compress (crane).

At first, the drill is done with legs only, so you can focus on things like physical alignments, correct technique, breathing (don't hold your breath!), and power. The key focus is watching when you Compress and Expand, and how you express them properly. As you progress, add in drunken cup fist guards (keeping hands and arms relaxed and in motion, "tending the bar" or spiraling), sloshing for power, target changes, changes in pivoting, and broken timing. There are many additional drunken skillsets to layer on to this simple drill, but must be done so methodically and conscientiously in order to actually be effective drunken boxing.

DAILY DOSE: Train several lines of this front-side kick combination to really study the Compress + Expand dynamic. Only add in additional elements once the previous ones are really internalized, then train them repetitively, accordingly.

A more advanced continuation of the above kicking drill begins in the same way, then adds more complexity.

1.   2.   3.

4.   5.   6.

Facing south again, the first three motions are the same: 1. Compress (crane), 2. Expand (front kick), 3. Expand further (side kick). 4. The sidekick pulls / hooks back to a crane stance (compress), this time without pivoting, so you remain facing east. Hands cross in front, right in front of left. 5. Stomp down to a low *mabu*, hands opening on their respective sides as fists, pounding an imaginary waist-level surface (expand). 6. The right foot remains in place while the left foot cross-steps behind to the south into a wide X-stance. As this is done, both cup fists swing horizontally to the north, adding to the twisting / coiling dynamic (compress).

7.   8.   9.

10.   11.   12.

7. Now the left foot remains in place as the right foot heavily sweeps in a large arc along the ground towards the south. Cup fists swing horizontally to the south with a slightly staggered timing (expand). 8. Cup fists guards remain facing south as the right leg draws up to crane stance (compress), before 9. stomping down to a high X-stance (meaning the toes of the right foot are turned to the west). 10. This foot positioning is the trajectory set up for the next kick, which is a roundhouse kick targeting the south (expand). The pathway of this kick is unique, in that it changes direction partway through, drilling the concept of multi-dimensional strikes. 11. As the horizontal swing of the kick is just before the southern direction, it plummets dramatically and "kicks" the ground right near the right foot, the left foot facing north from the spin of the kick. Hands cross in front close to the chest, drawing into the diameter of the body to increase the spin of the centripetal force (compress). If actually

stopping at this point, you'd be in a modified nail stance. 12. The energy from "kicking" into the ground bounces up and is transferred into the opposite leg, which continues the spinning momentum and does a spinning reverse roundhouse to the south (expand).

13.   14.   15.

13. As the kicking heel strikes to the south, the leg is quickly drawn back to a crane stance, dissipating the momentum of the spinning kick, stopping the body as it faces south (compress). Hands are in double cup fist guards facing south, right hand in front to match the raised right knee of the crane stance. 14. The right foot heavily steps down in front with the toes facing west, and 15. the entire body sinks low into a low X-stance. Simultaneously, the cup fists do a splitting strike: left fist towards the south, down at a 45-degree angle, and the right fist up at a 45-degree angle towards the north. The motion of the sink into the stance and the strike ends at exactly the same time (stance: compress, hands: expand). From here, the motions then

repeat on the opposite side (front kick from the X stance), effectively creating lines to be trained up and down your training space.

There is a lot going on with this pattern, and there are multiple qualities to train within it, beyond just "compress" and "expand". However, things such as sloshing, broken timing, heaviness, lightness, spirals, swaying, multi-dimensional strikes and blocks, and so on, should only be included once the standard shapes are correctly expressed with compression and expansion.

As previously mentioned, many drunken forms showcase staccato "drinks" as the player leans back, sometimes staggering the motion or just repeating it. This is an indication of how Compression & Expansion and Broken Timing can be integrated into such strikes, but it's all too easy to get lost in the theatrics or try to rush the acquisition of such abilities. As with any drunken fist training, without solid fundamentals and conscientious practice patterns, it comes crashing down pretty quickly, and in an ugly way.

行停無跡伸曲潛踪

"Whether moving or pausing, your intentions are hidden"
-Drunken Fist Saying

Other considerations are that the variations of the above combination are numerous, and can be found throughout any valid traditional drunken forms. The Compress & Expand dynamic doesn't have to be restricted to "only kicking" or "only punching" pairs, and in fact works best if employed using the entire body's weapons arsenal. The reason that your teacher wants you to internalize a form and its plethora of multifaceted movements is so that you can ultimately string them together as appropriate, executing them using drunken methods like those outlined here, deceiving others with distance, timing, and power. Only then can you be a dangerous challenge to your opponents, only then can you be an effective drunken boxer, and only then can you "*be like mist*".

"The fists express from the central column, and the strikes are like smoke. The body is that of a madman; steps and movements obscuring east from west, north from south."

-Drunken Fist Adage

STRETCHING, YOUR DRUNKEN BUDGET
Suppleness and Flexibility are Life: Bamboo
by Ma Hao Xing

"Zui Quan reflects many of the core concepts of ditangquan *or "ground boxing", as its adepts very much adhere to the proper principles of falling and rolling. In fact, some schools posit that Drunken Boxing's origins trace back to certain schools of dog boxing / ground boxing, and then branched off to form a separate, distinct style. Poems and scriptures of the style's origin reference "the earth's dragons" forming the foundations of its attacks, and the "entire body manifesting hidden strength and savvy". Such songs / poems were made for easier transmission and retention of the fundamental concepts of a style. Simple, easy-to-memorize verses helped ensure, at the very least, the key-words of a style were not lost to time." – Zui Quan Discourse*

How do drunken boxers achieve the feeling of water rising up, pouring through the limbs and striking an adversary, throwing heavy, rubbery weight around like swift currents move in a river? Keeping physicality flexible and muscles pliable means that the body is resilient, so strength can extend and recoil throughout the body. While even large trees flex in a severe wind, bamboo's resilience and suppleness in this situation is most apparent. Stretching, strengthening, relaxing, flexibility, pliability, are vital constituents before starting any style worth learning. It should be made clear that warmups should not be random, rather, they should be the *gongfu* itself. The stretching and warmups should consist of the foundations and actual martial arts of the style, used as a means to break in the body and compile physical attributes to enhance learning the stages of the art. Philosophically and practically, stretching and warmups are the *gongfu*: they are not separate. The actual end goal of the practice is creating a vessel that is stronger, longer, denser, more watery, more resilient and limber. Naturally occurring athletic ability can only carry one so far, and fades over time as one ages. Correct *gong* at the early stages leads to longevity, life strength, and inner power that does not diminish. Seek training that provides residual internal power built into your structure over time. Your older self will thank you when you're not feeble and you've retained some rejuvenating power as you gracefully age. Whether you concertedly seek this now or not, it's the essence of what these arts provide. Early stages of training build up the body, and one way to make the process more streamlined is employing martial calisthenics when warming up, cooling down, or stretching. Not only do martial calisthenics secure tendon strength and invigorate the body, they result in the long-term internal power one seeks from training.

Attend to your spine, your hips, your ankles and shoulders. Particularly as one ages, these areas fall into neglect. Specific strengthening and stretching patterns are found within all traditional lineages that have drunken sets, or in manuals like *The Path of Drunken Boxing* (Eight Immortals sets, akin to *tian gan* (heavenly stem) training sets, but distinctively for drunken fist).

翻滚跌撲

"Rolling and tumbling."

Crawling, rolling, and falling motions are necessary, regardless of athletic prowess. Why? Quadrupedal motion develops core endurance as it keeps the torso under continuous isometric tension. Rotational power trained by doing things like "lizard walking" or "shoulder walking" translates well into activities such as *shuai jiao* or certain kicking techniques, among others. Further, the capacity developed for maintaining strength over longer time periods is the type of endurance one needs for *zui quan*. Basically, the wider range of motion cultivated by such activity assists with injury prevention, increased mobility, proprioception, balance, and overall athletic ability.

DAILY DOSE: Stretch your spine: do bridges, arches, "superman stretches". This is not just for if you plan on acrobatics and kip ups, it's for flossing your vertebrae, keeping CSF flowing, and maintaining the machine.

Sit in a low squat position as often as feasible, as this aids the ankles, hips and spine. Engage in any activity or position that opens your hips and *kua*. Rollers, balls, and rods can be good for working at knotted or gamey areas. Breathe into and through the stretches.

If you have a partner, have them slowly – slowly – put on shoulder locking *qin na* techniques and hold them at pinnacle range, effectively using *qin na* to act as a "partner stretching drill." Keep shoulder sockets lubricated with lots of motion throughout the day.

Engage in animal movements, such as bear walking, monkey running, lizard crawling, crab walking, shoulder walking, butt / hip walking, and rolling around. Make these a serious part of your warmup / cool-down patterns.

Do many forward, backward, and sideways rolls, as well as breakfalls, as the benefits are myriad. Don't be afraid to fall or be tossed.

SLEEPING IT ALL OFF
Strategic Lying Around to Achieve Progress
from discussions with Zhu Yingyu

Something often overlooked or neglected in the training discussion is the topic of sleep. Without adequate rest, one cannot truly reap the benefits of intense training. Part of this process is having a *schedule*, just like any other good habit. Just as you make time and have regularity with your physical routine, you need to be just as vigilant with your slumber. It's funny, because a lot of this is easier said than done for something that is so paramount to progress and skill development.

Another aspect that gets neglected is the actual sleep *environment*. The bedroom should be a place of quiet and serenity, a place to recharge and settle at the end of the day. The bedroom should not be your office, nor should it be your gaming area, nor should it be a place of socializing. Keep it as a sanctuary, even if that sounds like a platitude. Resolve to have it as a place of *peace*.

Cortisol and growth hormone are components of proper rest. Growth hormone is necessary for increased musculature and physical strength, as well as for speeding up healing after injuries and training.

Getting adequate rest also lowers stress hormones like cortisol in the body and recalibrates and balances the "thermostat" of the internal mechanisms. Over-stress and intense training result in inflammation, which in turn leads to nagging injuries in the short-term, and long-term ailments as well. Many chronic and acute injuries are actually avoidable with enough sleep. Train hard, and then sleep it off. Sleep is genuinely a critical component of intelligent training, especially for those at the higher levels along the drunken fist experience.

THE BODY CLOCK

It would be remiss to discuss sleep and not delve into the concept of the Chinese body clock and organ functions as well. The body naturally follows circadian rhythms, helping to regulate eating patterns, temperature, digestion, and cleansing. Energy's cyclical ebb and flow throughout the body is seen as following a 24-hour pattern, with two-hour intervals focusing on specific organ systems. Put simply, energy draws inward during sleep to deal with restorative functions, and moves outward again during waking phases, which include digestion and elimination. Transition between the two occurs between 1 and 3 am, at which point the liver engages in a variety of important functions such as cleaning the blood, thereby adjusting the body for the outward phase of the cycle. Peak

function of the liver is followed by a 12-hour span dealing with

absorption, digestion and elimination – the lungs, large intestine,

stomach / pancreas, heart, and small intestine. The subsequent time

frame, starting in the afternoon, moves towards maintenance and

restorative functions: the pericardium, triple burner, bladder /

kidneys and the liver.

Time Interval	System
3 – 5 am	Lung
5 – 7 am	Large Intestine
7 – 9 am	Stomach
9 – 11 am	Spleen
11 am – 1 pm	Heart
1 – 3 pm	Small Intestine
3 – 5 pm	Bladder
5 – 7 pm	Kidney
7 – 9 pm	Pericardium
9 – 11 pm	Triple Burner
11 pm – 1 am	Gall Bladder
1 – 3 am	Liver

	Metal
	Earth
	Fire
	Wood
	Water

Essentially, it's an outline of a daily maintenance and repair timeline

which can offer insight as to excesses and deficiencies in your

overall system. Certain windows of fatigue or lethargy can be

examined according to which organ and meridian set may need

attending to. As a further example, it also correlates with why deep breathing exercises like *qigong* are often suggested to be done at dawn, as the lungs are considered at optimal functionality between 3 and 5 am.

So, whether subscribing to western or eastern medicine perspectives, all the experts agree that sleep is important. While it's quite ironic that a high-level martial art like drunken fist is associated with inebriation, in actuality, the long-term goal is achieving high levels of balance in terms of health, mindset, and physicality. Diet, calisthenics, meditation, *qigong*, *neigong*, and natural medicines all play a role in this. Critical, then, is incorporating a regular sleep schedule as part of the training, not simply collapsing into bed exhausted at the end of a training session. As a caveat to the above discourse on the body clock: like any theory, it's important to read the "warning label" on the bottle, and not get too hung up on the concept at the expense of the practice. In other words....don't lose sleep over the little details, just get yourself to bed.

DAILY DOSE: Make a sleep schedule and stick to it, prioritizing it as a necessary component for your training and recovery.

QI

DEEP BREATHS,
DEEP RELATIONSHIPS

QI

While the concept of *qi* applies to a vast array of phenomena within the broad context of Chinese culture— from weather, to philosophy, to emotions, to medicine — to name a few, the main usage in this text is within the framework of *breath*, and how it bridges the relationship between the physical body and spiritual expression of an individual's *gong fu*. Breath is the vital life force that imbibes us with life and energy, so controlling its methods and relationship to the self can unlock a great deal of potential.

Qigong, as a moving practice, is the cusp of the relationship between the physical and the ethereal. It informs the body's motions, and guides towards correct posture and physicality. In turn, once the body settles into these correct parameters, one can become more fully aware of internal phenomena, without having the distractions of attending to shapes and the physical body. Physical shapes of the training should not be a diversion, rather, they should conduct the practitioner towards inner movements and sensations. Thus, our *qi* is an examination of this *relationship*.

Intermediate training brings intent into the form, where mind and breath are combined together. Dynamic openings of the body are explored, and we begin to see how power is manifested through the shapes. At this phase of progress the *yi* (intent) and *qi* (breath) are the focus of training.

There is a Daoist concept that posits the slower the breath, the longer the life of the organism. One interpretation is that each living thing is imbibed with a set number of inhalations and exhalations beginning at birth, which is like a clock ticking down until we pass on. As such, keeping a steady and slower breathing tempo extends the time we have in this existence. Respiration in trees is extended and slowly paced, directly coinciding with their prolonged lifespans. In contrast, smaller animals like mice breathe at a rapid pace, displaying a faster decline and living for much shorter periods. While generally oversimplified, the concept is easily grasped, and actually has overlap with scientific elements. Deep, controlled, and habitual breathing lowers stress hormones, removes waste, lowers blood pressure, and results in a whole plethora of positive health benefits. No matter how you view it, having awareness and control of one's breath is vital for robust *qi*.

WHERE IS MY MIND?
Drunk Body, Sober Mind

from discussions with Zhang Jing Fa & Wei Laoshi

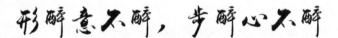

"Drunken physicality, sober mind"

– Drunken Fist Saying

Literally: "The shape / form is drunk, the intent is not. The steps are drunk, the heart / mind is not"

Breath is a connection between the outside environment and the inner workings of your body. This is one relationship of breathing. It is also a connection between your physical being – the structures of the respiration apparatus and chemical exchanges – and one's state of mind at a given moment. Breathing can both calm and excite you, so maintaining awareness and control of your respiratory mechanisms is a necessary component for the relationship between how you feel and react. *Zui Quan* requires a solid command of this interconnection.

While theatrics are indeed a component of *zui quan*, it's very easy to get too focused or caught up in the performative nature of the movements, losing sight of the actual nature of the style.

You must be the chaos of the storm (various stages and depictions of drunkenness), while simultaneously being the calm center of the storm (calm and attentive mindset, focused on the combat at hand).

斟酒 。 初飲 。 微醉 。 顛狂醉 。 爛醉 。 醒酒 。 宿醉

The spectrum of drunkenness – from least to most – is one aspect of the mind training of drunken style *gong fu*. This is not done so in order to solicit a reaction like, "Oh no! The guy that I'm fighting just suddenly became 20% drunker!" Instead, just as one can always continue to reach deeper levels of relaxation, other states or qualities can also similarly be enhanced. The different phases of drunkenness are used to impart distinct qualities to how one moves, reacts, attacks, and defends. Think of it as how you could have different levels of ferocity, or relaxation, or calmness, or anger; things are a spectrum, not a binary. The phases of drunkenness listed above are:

1 斟酒   2 初飲   3 微醉   4 顛狂醉   5 爛醉   6 醒酒   7 宿醉

1. Pouring wine 2. Early drinks 3. Slightly / Happy drunk (Tipsy) 4. Wildly drunk
5. Completely blackout drunk 6. Sobering up 7. Hungover

Another lineage's variation of this categorization is: **Playful, Covetous, Friendly, Sober, Sick**

Playful drunks keep relaxed via games, trickery, being mischievous and engaging in "humor", focused on playful antics that embarrass or distract an opponent. **Covetous** drunks are intent on not sharing the wine, keeping it "protected" and out of reach of an adversary. **Friendly** drunks insist on sharing the alcohol, bridging via handshakes, shoulder grips and hugs, getting the "drinking buddy" "caught up in the gears" as he's forcibly dragged into the drinking of the wine. **Sober** drunks are how you feel at the end of a bender, hungover and surly, much more aggressive and direct, much more willing to devastate a challenger and eliminate what bothers you. **Sick** drunks are known to convulse (shaking, destructive *qin na*), "fall asleep" (dead weight methods), "go blind" (mental games, vital point strikes), and "heal" others (forcing "medicine" ingestion, examinations, acupoint strikes), being a very distinct form of this *quan*.

There is clearly a similar logic and implementation of these groupings between lineages. Overall, the premise remains the same: seek qualitative difference in the conveyance of your *quan*, ensuring that you're able to distinctly display each in effective ways. The outer physicality of these should range from somewhat impacted to completely out of control. How you confidently express these is part of your *Shen*, which essentially hinges upon how properly and confidently you've assimilated your boxing skills. In other words, learning drunken fist isn't going to magically teach you how to do a proper throw or takedown – these are abilities and skills that you should have already refined and perfected before learning these methods. Instead, drunken boxing approaches are meant to alter the qualities and execution of existing skillsets, thereby rendering them less predictable and more dangerous.

"Confuse opponents"
– Drunken Fist Adage

Confusion exists in many ways. The scale of drunken mindsets is a tool for exploring relationships and continuums, and expressing them through your own spirit. "Confusion" that arises in an opponent is a by-product of solidly integrated martial skills, not the result of simply tricking them with drunken melodramatics. Hone your skillsets, sharpen your blades, further distill your wine.

SITTING & DOING

An Outline of Some Basic *Gong Fu* and Drunken Meditations

by Zhang Jing Fa

While it may seem strange to quantify and categorize a type of personal and internal work like meditation, it often helps with beginner students or even teachers to see a framework of potential avenues of exploration. As you progress, there can be overlap in methodologies, but when starting out it's best to keep things simple and separate. As per usual with such things, more complex or advanced meditations should be explored only with experienced guidance of a qualified instructor. That said, below are several general descriptions of different meditation methods, and each is followed with how these can be explored in one's *zui quan* training.

Remember that posture is incredibly important. Seek balance in the spine so you can release the body and rely on its structural integrity. Especially when starting out, it's a good idea to have a physical checklist of how to approach alignment: *baihui*, *dazhui*, *mingmen*, and *huiyin* are effectively in a straight line. This allows for muscularity to relax as much as possible. If unfamiliar with these locations, this is a simplification:

- *baihui*: reach through top of head, release everything underneath, opening the base of the skull (the latter sometimes called the "jade pillow").
- *dazhui*: large vertebrae at the cervical root.
- *mingmen*: between kidneys, pull gently
- *huiyin*: tuck the pelvis / tailbone, opens the spinal column via traction downwards and upwards, increasing CSF flow, releasing undue tension.

Discover a seated posture that can be held for reasonable lengths of time without experiencing cramping, numbness, or pain. You need to remove as much physicality from the equation so that you can keep your attention on the internal work. "Seek release in the physical". A principle from traditional Chinese medicine is that the mind and body are one; we treat the mind to treat the body, and we treat the body to treat the mind. Proper meditation is medication.

1. OBSERVING THE BREATH

The basic process of meditating is simply returning to meditating. Your mind strays, so you'll continually re-focus your attention on your breath. Over time, the distractions become less frequent and intense, and you become more proficient and deeper with your practice.

METHOD: From a comfortable, seated position, eyes are closed and the focus is on the inhalation-exhalation cycle. Your checklist is: good posture, tongue raised to your upper palate, and breathing in through the nose. Pay attention to the breath drawing in, deep into the lungs into the lower tips of the lobes. Oxygen is brought fully into the lungs without straining; full, yet relaxed. Observe the pace of even in- and out-breaths, continually returning to this cycle if your mind wanders. Some traditions say to breathe out via the mouth, others say the nose is fine. Regardless, the key is staying attentive to deep, rhythmic breathing for several minutes, gradually adding time as your skill advances.

As inevitable external distractions arise (such as a car horn in the distance, a neighbor's crying child, etc.), simply "label" the distraction and let it drift away. Some visualize such distractions as clouds drifting away from the mind, allowing them to pass without energizing them with focus and engagement. Others think of a gently flowing river, and the thoughts are leaves and debris that float away. Whichever method suits you best, the key is allowing distracting thoughts and stimuli to continue onwards, away from you. As you focus and fixate on a thought, it gains energy and grows, taking root. The method is to train the mind to let it go before it begins this process.

ZUI QUAN **APPROACH:** Having the breathing apparatus act as a rhythmic bellows is a necessary skill. The diaphragm expanding and contracting in a steady manner, expelling impurities and revitalizing the blood is a fundamental starting point. As relaxation is a vital spectrum to be explored and utilized in Drunken Fist, this meditation can be used as such: Mind sober, body drunk. "Relax the meat, soften the chatter". A variant of this is visualizing the breath as wine flowing in and out, slow and viscous with deep, penetrating effects. Simply watch it enter and leave without judgements, observing but not attaching to its influence. Breathe wine.

2. CONCENTRATION MEDITATION

Sometimes referred to as "block breathing" or "box breathing", the idea with this approach is to count your in and out breaths, staying occupied with the process and noticing phenomena which result from doing so. As above, sensations that arise are only observed, not focused on.

METHOD: Comfortably seated in good posture with the tongue raised to the upper palate, begin nasal breathing. A good starting point is slowly inhaling for a count of four, pausing for two, exhaling for four, then pausing for two, all done without tension or straining. This creates a rhythm for your respiration, along with a focal point while you calm your mind. As you advance, you can extend the inhalation / exhalation / pausing times, with some common patterns being 6-3-6-3, 8-3-8-3, or 8-4-8-4. As you practice, notice the sensations of the different and distinct sections: "filling" with air, pausing and being "full" of air, "emptying" of air, and pausing as you are "empty" of air. Really observe and pay attention to each phase's unique aspects.

There is the paradox that as you fill with air, your body becomes "emptier" (in the sense that the lungs, like balloons, become emptier with more space inside when inflated), and when you exhale, your body is "fuller", in that it's more physically dense. If you're invested in Drunken Fist training, or any substantial *gong fu* / martial arts methodologies, you're aware of theories involving *Yin-Yang* and *Yin-Yang* reversal. We can use this type of meditation to refine our empirical cognition of the extreme reach of *Yin* changing to *Yang*, or vice versa.

We do this by ascribing either "*Yin*" or "*Yang*" to the inhalation or exhalation. It can be either one, depending on how you decide to view the paradox above. "*Yin*" is usually "emptying" and "receiving", whereas "*Yang*" is "full" and "giving". As an example, we'll associate "*Yin*" with exhaling, as we "empty" the air, and "*Yang*" with inhaling as we "fill". As you inhale, imagine your mind tracing a circle around the outside of the classic *Taijitu* / *Yin-Yang* diagram on the white yang fish. As you reach capacity, you're now at the top of the circle where the "dot" (remnant of yin) is. The brief holding of the breath is the moment where *Yang* becomes *Yin*, represented by this dot. As you exhale, imagine your mind tracing down the dark "*Yin*" fish of the diagram, becoming darker as you empty of air. When you've fully exhaled, you're at the extreme aspect of *Yin*, which reverses back into *Yang*.

Of course, this transition from empty to full, *Yin* to *Yang* might seem obvious to some, but the purpose is to explore the transformation *process* from one to another, carefully observing how these changes feel and relate to each other. Pay attention to internalizing the *Yin-Yang*, even visualizing the diagram as part of your body (for example, white *Yang* is the spine (*du mai*, conception vessel), follow the breath upwards as you inhale. Black *Yin* is the front (*ren mai*, governing vessel), follow the breath downwards as you exhale). As transitions between *Yin* and *Yang* are vital components of drunken fist, becoming acutely aware of how they express can help your training immensely.

ZUI QUAN APPROACH: Rather than breath, visualize yourself filling with wine. While it's still the ebb and flow of *yin-yang* reversals, we use wine as our focus rather than breath. It's a slower, thicker, heavier substance which requires more mental acuity to control, which is a necessary component of *zui quan*. The *taijitu* / *yin-yang* diagram can also be seen as a gourd, one side white, one

black. Your "wine" flows up and down within the gourd, changing from light to dark and light to heavy as it does so. YOU become the gourd; the breath is your wine. Both metaphorically and literally, the wine is what fuels you and keeps you fighting. We don't fixate on the wine, we observe the transitions and sensations of each of the four phases herein: Filling, Full, Emptying, Empty. This visualization meditation dovetails perfectly with certain sloshing training, outlined elsewhere in this book.

3. WALKING MEDITATION

A well-ventilated room free of obstacles and distractions is the ideal setting. I've explored several methods of walking meditation, but the one with the most profound (and ironically) quickest tangible results, is the one with the slowest movement. As you stand with your feet shoulder-width apart, feel gravity pulling your weight down through your legs and feet. In this way, your weight is evenly distributed, and in effect, "nothing" is happening. Now, if you slightly lean to one side, for example, your right, as you do so you'll feel your weight shift into your right foot as the pressure in your left foot diminishes. Your right foot is now "fuller" than your left, the latter of which is now "emptier". If you slowly shift from right to left and back again, paying attention to this weight shifting, you'll experience the process of "filling" and "emptying" in each foot, as well as different *parts* of each foot. In fact, you'll experience a four-step process akin to the "Concentration Meditation" described above: Filling, Full, Emptying, Empty. The difference with this is that this process coincides with empirical weight changes in the body, as well as movement forward (once we begin the actual walking meditation).

METHOD: Best results are achieved if done shortly after waking up, done with an empty stomach, save for some water to rehydrate after sleeping. With correct postural alignment and tongue placement, fix a soft gaze straight ahead towards the horizon. Your focus is not on a forward, distant point. Rather, you open up your peripheral views and expand feeling all around you in a sphere. Hands have two options: one is leaving them hanging loosely at your sides. The other is one hand lightly grasping the other as both cover your lower belly region. When starting out, leave hands hanging loosely.

Bellows breathing, deep into the lungs without any strain or stress, keeps your breathing soft and regular and offers rhythmic breath exchange. However, the focus is not your breath. You're going to walk forward at an **extremely** slow pace, observing the sensations of the weight exchange in the soles of your feet. The slower the better, and the pace of movement should remain constant, as though drawing silk. To give an example, our group used to only cover a distance of a few meters after an hour of practice. It goes without saying that this is not a race; this is a deep exploration of the physical sensation of this *yin-yang* reversal. The distance between your steps is minimal: the mid-point of your foot only steps forward about the distance of your other foot's toes.

As one foot is "emptying", the other is "filling", these two sensations occurring simultaneously. At the apex, one is "full" while the other is "empty", until the cycle continues. Despite such slow movement, your balance is also challenged as you explore the tiny adjustments made to maintain your upright position. Along with this, you re-adjust your nervous system to a slower pace. If your mind wanders during your wandering, just bring your focus back to your feet. It's easy to lose track of time once you really get into depth with this practice, so it's good to set a timer. Start with 20 minutes, and work your way up to longer sessions. Upon finishing your inner work, be sure to use a form of "closing" from *qigong* to properly end the meditation interval.

ZUI QUAN APPROACH: After doing the above walking meditation for a set period of time, stop and stand with your feet shoulder-width apart. Without stepping, shift your weight in slow circles, examining the sensation of this "emptying-filling" process in the various parts of your feet. Circle clockwise, counter-clockwise, and even feet in opposite directions, moving just as slowly and methodically as when you were walking forward. As mentioned in other writings about Drunken Fist, deeply understanding the transitions and cycles of *yin-yang* reversal is critical to proper physical and mental expression of the art. Imagine wine slowly swirling around inside of a hollow gourd, feeling how the subtle weight shifts move and affect you.

4. VISUALIZATION MEDITATION

Put a gourd or glass on the floor in front of you. Ponder the potentials and feelings as though YOU were the vessel: what it's made of, its empty / full paradox (full of wine means empty of potential or air, empty of wine means full of potential or air.), how it feels to swirl and slosh the liquid inside, expand awareness to all around. This intertwines well with the physical practice of drunken sloshing. As with all sitting and breathing, practice the principles, but don't attach to ideas, sensations and results. Soften and observe.

TESTING YOUR BREATH
The Science of Breath Control
by Huang Dekui

The struggles with life's stresses are very real, and to deal with them, we must change the physiology of the body through proper energization. One must energize the self: breathing deeper and longer, meditating, engaging the body with movement – all things that radically affect biochemistry. Part of the greatness of modern times is the ability to craft bridges with the past, so ancient wisdom is now being confirmed with modern science: the two are not adversarial, they are complementary. The path that the mind takes under stress is highly influenced by training. Ancients knew that **the mind controls the body, which in turn leads the body to control the mind**, so controlling this relationship through informed practice is key. Many recent studies confirm this viewpoint, being able to study the physicality and the chemistry of the body in ways previously unavailable.

Our bodies have built-in mechanisms that can both increase and decrease stress. The nervous system controls *arousal*, essentially referring to our *alertness* set in contrast to our *calmness*. This balance or imbalance determines what we sense, how we think, what we perceive, and how we act. Put another way: how we exist in the world hinges upon our equilibrium between alertness and calmness. Because states of extreme stress are not at all ideal for most functioning and overall sense of well-being, it makes sense that one would attempt to adapt and regulate the stress system. It would make even more sense to have a systemized approach to this.

As alertness increases, due to both positive and negative stimuli, our senses massively focus: pupils dilate and our auditory system locks in, causing us to fixate on whatever we're perceiving to be important in that context. In essence, stress results in tunnel vision, and tunnel hearing. In the opposite realm, being relaxed means that it's much easier to absorb and process information.

THE MIND CONTROLS THE BODY, THE BODY CONTROLS THE MIND

There is really a simple and basic relationship between the movement of the diaphragm, the lungs, and the heart, as well as neural signals from the brain. There's no need to delve into any sort of mystifying discourse, as controlling the physical mechanisms of respiration alone can result in positive changes to biochemistry and well-being.

The breathing muscle, the diaphragm, is situated below the heart, and moves the lungs as it contracts, moving downward with inhalation. When one breathes in, the space in the chest cavity becomes larger, and the lungs expand into it. Muscles situated between the ribs also assist with expanding the chest cavity, contracting to pull your rib cage both upward and outward during inhalation. There is a crucial relationship between *how* we breathe, and our states of arousal.

INHALING MAKES YOU MORE ALERT, EXHALING CALMS YOU

INHALE: When the lungs are expanded during exhalation, it creates more space for the heart, thereby slowing blood flow. This, in turn, leads to a signal from the brain to speed up the heart rate. As a shorthand: increased heart rate can be achieved by inhaling more, with inhalations longer than exhalations. Increased alertness occurs by inhaling more than exhaling: deeper and longer. The mind controls the body (i.e., choosing longer breaths in), which in turn leads the body to control the mind (i.e., increased alertness). Controlling this relationship through practice is key.

EXHALE: During this process, the diaphragm moves up, making the lungs more contracted. This means less space for heart, thereby speeding up blood flow. As a reaction, the brain sends a signal to slow down the heart rate. In short: decreased heart rate can be achieved by exhaling more than inhaling: deeper and longer / lengthen exhales, with exhalations longer than inhalations. Relaxation is achieved by extending and deepening exhalations relative to inhalations.

With regard to one's relationship with autonomic arousal, breath control is the chance to reset things, so that when stressors are encountered, there's a buffer zone created. For the purposes of our *zui quan*, it's a "drunken state", which allows for more control of both physiology and mindset. Once repositioned to a lower setting, it's far easier to remain calm under duress. Three proven methods are outlined below, which can be done either comfortably seated or lying down. Inhale via the nose, exhale via the mouth.

1. PHYSIOLOGICAL SIGHS: The trigger to breathe is when increased levels of CO_2 are present in the bloodstream and lungs. When CO_2 gets too high in the system the body's response is the physiological sigh. It's a process that inflates the alveoli sacs in the lungs, and maximally offloads CO_2. If you've ever witnessed children sobbing and regaining their breath, it's this very thing. It's essentially a pattern of two quick inhales, followed by an exhale. It's unconsciously done in sleep, claustrophobic situations, and can be seen in animals as well.

DAILY DOSE: Pattern: Inhale- inhale -exhale. 5 minutes per day.

2. HYPERVENTILATION: Deep inhalations are done repetitively (not fast, just steady), paired with shallow exhalations for 35 to 40 breaths. It's common to feel lightheaded or dizzy while doing so, but this is just part of the process. Upon the last breath, fully empty the lungs (without straining), and hold for as long as possible in this exhale state, at least one minute. When you feel the need to breathe, inhale and hold for 20 seconds. This is one set.

DAILY DOSE: Pattern: Hyperventilate – exhale and hold – inhale and hold. 3 to 5 sets per day.

3. BOX BREATHING: For this method, one breathing cycle is divided into four parts: inhale, pause when full, exhale, pause when empty. The pauses are typically shorter than the breath exchange components, with a good starting pattern as 4 seconds, 2 seconds, 4 seconds, 2 seconds. Some other timings could be: 6-3-6-3, 8-3-8-3, or 8-4-8-4, ultimately depending on which approach feels best and doesn't cause undue strain while breathing.

DAILY DOSE: Pattern: Inhale – pause – exhale – pause. 5 minutes per day.

Essentially, all of the above are pathways to inoculate the self from stress, by methodically and mechanically inducing minor stress patterns. Changes in the heart rate and biochemistry help to recalibrate the nervous system to be comfortable in uncomfortable states. The utility to the above methods is that they're presented here as purely mechanical, meaning that you don't have to worry about chasing or accessing certain states of mind, checking where you're "supposed to be at". Rather, you follow a short, prescribed physical schedule, and the studies behind these methods demonstrate that the positive peripheral benefits just naturally occur.

"COMING DOWN (THE MOUNTAIN)"
Focus / Determination / Calmness / Clarity

by Lee Wei Xiao

This particular meditation became part of our practice to "sober up" after very "drunken" training. The slow, methodical "walk" down the mountain settles the mind, tunes the breath, and rebalances the nervous system to an un-drunken state. It's quite helpful at showing the differences in the two extremes.

Meditation is really about the continual return to meditating. The more one practices it, the more this is seen to be true, while at the same time, the better one becomes at it. Practice doesn't really make perfect; it just makes *better*...in incremental steps. As with other forms of mind training, over time, the mechanism contained within are internalized and become more a part of you.

INSTRUCTION:

Sit comfortably, posture aligned as you would when having to sit for a length of time. Having knees and shins touching the floor in a type of modified half-lotus, one heel tucked under the perineum, works

well for creating a foundation to rest the body's weight on (akin to yoga's *Siddhasana* or *Muktasana*). Slightly elevating the buttocks on a cushion helps align the spine naturally.

一 Sit with correct posture

二 Hands start palms together at the "peak" of the mountain (山) in the 合掌 / hé zhǎng position, (*"wai"* / Añjali Mudrā), above your head, shoulder blades back and down, no rising of the shoulders.

三 Eyes closed. Belly breathing, even paced.

四 Slowly lower hands, counting from 1 to 100. Hands will trace a triangle shape from the peak of the mountain to the base. As your hands separate, don't become distracted by the sensations between the palms or elsewhere in the body.

五 Keep an even pace (akin to drawing of silk), aiming to end with hands on thighs as you reach count of 100. The motion is slow and steady.

六 Breathe constantly. Deeply, without strain, into lower *dantian*.

七 Maintain focus on your count.

八 As you maintain movement and breath, you're able to sustain constant, deliberate, controlled movement.

酒 The mind settles from "drunken" to "sober" by the time you reach the base of the mountain.

DAILY DOSE: Include this after very sloppy, "drunken" sessions to regulate the drunken temperament.

WUXING RELATIONSHIPS
Theory and Action – Combat Map
by Ma Hao Xing

Invaluable to progress is finding the equilibrium between intellectualizing and actualizing, or finding proper *qi* for your *gong fu* mentality and physicality. Put another way, it's finding the balance between theory and practice. At the end of the day, it comes down to how you map out your approach to what is being trained.

五行

The *WuXing*, or five phases / elements, is a conceptual system that is juxtaposed over multiple aspects of Chinese culture, including those in the martial realm. Simply stated, it's a system of five phases outlining the relationships and interactions between various phenomena. Like all numerology in this culture, it's a method of categorizing things to aid in explanation and transmission of more complex ideas. Most commonly associated with "internal" arts such as *Xíngyìquán* or *Tàijíquán*, it has an underlying existence and influence in multiple other martial approaches as well.

This discussion expands upon the *wuxing* as it pertains to an overall combat strategy that was outlined by one of my *zui quan* teachers. Basically, the theory posits that success in combat is predicated upon understanding, execution, and fine-tuning of these fundamentals.

1. **Metal:** Access: distance, angles, timing
2. **Wood:** Control: position, grips, strikes
3. **Earth:** Stability: base, posture, structure
4. **Water:** Efficiency: stamina (not gassing out), energy, breathing
5. **Fire:** Strategy / Tactics: knowing when to be offensive vs. defensive

For those unfamiliar, the interior arrows depict the "destructive" cycle of the five elements, while the circular arrows around the perimeter indicate the "generative / creation" relationship. Martially, these sometimes represent positions / movements, techniques, or states of combat. As outlined here, they're a general map for all types of combative engagement, from one-on-one fighting, all the way to large scale warfare.

While it's all well and good to have an understanding of theories driving your martial arts practice, it's also very necessary to be able to actualize the ideas in real, tangible boxing exercises. Take, for example, angles. How do you train this? What does this mean? Why is this critical? At the very least, you should have some base drills you regularly visit in order to showcase the requisite capability to refine this vital skill. Like any skill, it should also have layers to its acquisition, which refers to having progressive training plans that dial-up difficulty as you move forward. It should be able to have other aspects like speed and power stripped away and still have utility. So, once again, how do you train this?

As a general example, let's use "bridging" / "entry" for analysis. Ideally, when you engage with an opponent, you'll be "cutting" one of his lines of power, having some sort of influence or effect on his structure or options. Coupled with speed and power, this can end skirmishes quickly, but for training purposes, we aim to explore the subtle details of these encounters in order to refine them. For drunken boxers, this is cultivating the wine in the gourd. Achieving an ideal angle while making and maintaining contact with an adversary sets you in a much better position for winning the tide of battle, limiting his options, and distilling what is most appropriate to next employ from your own attack arsenal. Depending on the circumstances, this can be done via head, torso, or limbs, although most commonly the latter is encountered first, due to proximity in conventional fighting methodology; limbs extend out furthest.

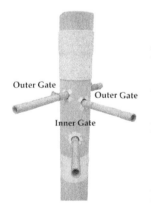

So, your partner attacks, and you end up with hands situated at his wrist and elbow, on the outer gate. Stop. Examine your feet, torso positioning, distances, pressures, etc. In this "snapshot", are you positioned such that you have an advantage? Are your lines of force / power / attack set up in such a way as to be a threat to your adversary? What options is he left with, or better yet, forced into?

Train with no power, as though both of you are made of glass, and any undue contact or pressure will shatter things. The focus is angles, not power. Find problem areas and adjust. Repeat. Until it becomes second-nature, examine this from the *WuXing* model above: How does your angle (metal) disrupt the opponent's position (wood)? How does this angle (metal) contribute to your own efficiency (water)? This is just part of the analysis for the *WuXing* concept, which can perhaps add new perspective or approach to training.

Given the odd quality of drunken boxing, the tidal wave nature of its heavy bridging often has multiple angles of pressure happening simultaneously or sequentially. That's not to say this can't happen in other disciplines, but drunken fist has this sloppy, heavy, burdensome feel that is quite apparent when on the receiving end of it. That said, the *angles* can still be explored while training with the *heaviness* removed.

Daily Dose: DUELING DRUNKARDS:
"Natural Fist" (*via the Red Jade school*)

One such drill that can be used for this is the "Duel" practice, sometimes labeled as a variation of *natural fist*. Partner X closes his eyes, and partner Y moves anywhere within striking range. The cue for Y to attack is when X opens his eyes, at which point X has to defend the attack. Y's attack is thrown as hard and fast as possible, which must be effectively dealt with by X. While this drill can be used for practicing many different skillsets, it's quite easy to simplify its aim as a bridging exercise to seek ideal angles. In this case, X doesn't need to use power or speed, as the goal is to simply respond with a viable placement / angle that seeks the upper hand in the positional game. It's easy to see how this drill could be used for other training agendas, such as speed, power, efficiency, structure, or particular strikes & responses. However, keeping practice focused on one, singular skill is usually much more productive, as it's quite easy to get lost in the excitement, turmoil, or ego of the moment. Having a training partner who is sympathetic to  similar goals is imperative to make this useful.

DAILY DOSE: This cannot be done enough, as there are so many layers that can be explored with this simple drill. Choose a parameter, and stay focused.

STANDING AROUND &
MINDING YOUR OWN BUSINESS
The *Qi* of *Zhan Zhuang*

from discussions with Zhang Jing Fa & Lin Guo Jie

In what way is your mental function harmonizing with your physical being? How this interplay occurs directly relates to the amount of tension and relaxation experienced while training. *Qi*, understood as a connection or affiliation, is the pivotal point between mental tuning and physical expression. Stationary exercises like various forms of *Zhan Zhuang* – standing post – help define this, while moving approaches such as *bu zhu gong fa* and *tian gan* explore this while in long, extended motions. While these are both necessary practices for examining exactly how much tension release is being manifested, the standing is often overlooked, or only touched upon in a cursory way.

This is not going to be an in-depth description of standing practice, as there are multiple resources readily available on the topic (granted, both good and bad). Instead, this is going to outline some "sound bites" as reminders as to why you should start, continue, or re-kindle your standing post program, and, more arguably more importantly, it's going to include certain tweaks and flourishes that should be included for Drunken Fist players who engage in the training.

TAKING A STAND

By its very nature, standing for any length of time necessitates that you find equilibrium between tension and relaxation, both in body and mind. Exhaustion stems from being overly tense, blown over by the wind and crumpling onto the floor results from being too loose. There is a constant feedback loop between the physical and the mental to achieve the perfect balance between this tense-relaxed nature, and the circulation fostered by such practices nourishes both the mind and body.

Just as *yinyang* is malleable and constantly changing, so is your own spectrum of *fang song* – relaxation – so you can never assume you've let go enough. Given its relatively *yin* nature, *zui quan* requires constant examination of what this feeling actually is. This is why standing practice is so vital for a drunken boxer: correct standing necessitates finding the continually shifting dynamic of tension and relaxation in order to remain standing upright for extended periods of time. It's a way of adapting in real time to pressures of the environment, in a slow enough dynamic for your mind to explore what's happening. During the throes of a drunken form or combat, this type of investigation is less likely, so the aim of *Zhan Zhuang* is to find a quiet focused activity that will eventually "reset" your relaxation parameters for when you engage in these more rigorous endeavors. Simply put, you want the relaxation gained from standing practice to seep into other activities, particularly your drunkard's boxing.

STANDING TREATMENT: POSTURE AS MEDICINE

Standing practice really opens you up, expanding joints, releasing tension areas, and tuning mental processes in a practical way. Consider it as a type of tonic or medicine, as it clearly prioritizes connections and processes within the structure to keep it as efficiently stable as possible.

Traditional medicine involves a holistic approach, seeing a strong connection between the emotions and internal organs, with any imbalance or irregularity clearly reflected in the latter. Regular standing regimens imitate the effects of practices such as cupping or acupuncture, without being invasive, and some people find the results even more profound and lasting than other treatments. Every component part of the training assists in integrating the mind into your tissues, and helps in being better able to use your body in terms of mechanics and structure. Connectivity is achieved from top to bottom, and it helps with better transference of physical power and leverage from the lower to the upper limbs. As you elongate the spine and recruit balanced musculature to maintain its position, discs decompress and the nervous system settles down. Relatively gentle practices like this also stimulate flow within, cleansing the body via better circulation of cerebrospinal fluid, lymph, and blood.

Some general advice to integrate into your practice includes:

- Like any internal or meditative work, don't chase results, and don't become attached to sensations, good or bad. Just do.

- Weight distribution on the feet is something to explore and adjust, and has larger effects than you think. Patience is a large part of achieving results with this training. Just be patient, and do.

拳如石，臂似繩

"Arm like a rope, fist like a stone." – Drunken Fist Concept

A well-known axiom within drunken boxing is about having your arm pliable like a rope, while your fist strikes like a stone. If these hard and soft qualities are seen as polarities, one aim of standing practice is to coalesce into the middle ground of both. One of the reasons applied drunken fist feels so heavy, is that its players are adept at physically releasing tension, which is also an expression of the mental aspect of practicing. You can't have a relaxed physical vessel while harboring a tense mind. This duality is constantly changing and evolving, and one's placement on the "relaxation spectrum" does as well. You can always be *more* relaxed, be it mental or physical.

First, the physical. One component of standing post practices, is that they necessitate the connection throughout the appendages and to the *dantian*. Correct structure and maximal relaxation are required for extended standing sessions, so it's a method that can't be faked; if you put the time in, the results become apparent. Over time, the removal of tension throughout the arms and torso creates a dynamic whereby the power generated in the center of the body uses the limbs as a channel for expressing force. A well-trained drunken player's strikes feel extremely dense, which stems from being able to remove tension and express through unimpeded connectivity.

The mental component is usually trickier. Naturally, the "monkey mind" that pops up in all forms of meditation and physical practice needs to be settled, but there's more than this. Different types of "drunk" necessitate different mindsets: "angry", "happy", "hungover", "sick", various "Eight Immortals". Each has its own mental characteristics, and each is trained while doing standing exercises. However, it needs to be stated that thoughts will never be fully extinguished, so the exercise is actually just about continuously returning to the practice while engaged in it. The more it is done, the easier such a mechanism becomes, but it's a common misconception that the mind remains constantly blank. This is the ideal, but the practice is the *process*, not the actual attainment.

STRIKING & THE MIND

Standard *Zui Quan* striking is not about "hitting" or "kicking" in the customary sense. Heavy motions are made, and incidental objects in the way of these motions feel the impact. An early preconception is to get rid of the idea that you're "kicking" or "hitting", in the orthodox way. This must be achieved systematically, however, and part of that methodical approach is standing practice. *Zhan Zhuang* training is what builds the structural framework through which power flows, and also tones the nervous system to calm the mind while under minor duress.

MOVING

As an aside – and tandem to this – it's useful to have a sort of moving practice as well, to continually receive feedback on how well the structure is holding up, and when you need to "draw back" and rebuild. This is a form of testing your progress. A solid, Heavy Hands / 鐵沙掌 / Iron Palm routine is a good next step, progressing to light work on a heavy bag, before ultimately working on full-power movements and strikes on the same. Counterintuitively, going slower through these stages actually leads to faster progress.

Once you start into actually moving, the concentration is on ***sloshing***, which is letting the internal wine sensation carry your motions. For a tangible way to feel this, find a large water container, such as a jug or bucket, and half-fill it with water. Covering with a lid keeps the liquid contained as you move it around your training space. Hug the container against your chest as you start to move around and "activate" the water inside, occasionally stopping your body to feel the movement of the liquid and how it sways and carries you. Naturally, you'll want to play around with the entire spectrum of large and small movements, exploring the realm of gross and subtle, all the while maintaining respectable structural alignments. The latter is both for power generation and safety. A drunken body – during both combat and practice – should feel like a heavy bag filled with swirling liquid, sloshing around, engulfing and impacting its environment. *Zui Quan* is a storm, continuously in motion, with great potential for destruction. Anything unfortunate enough to be in the path of the tempest is consumed and flung about recklessly.

One way to train is following a standard "bell curve", beginning and ending with smaller and subtle effects, reserving on working extreme and "floppy" movements during the middle period of your workout routine. My teacher would always say "鬆鬆的. . . 越鬆越好" ("Loose and relaxed, the more the better") mid-workout.

A useful goal for initial stages of martial training is to eliminate the dichotomy of body and mind. Naturally, early training consists of observation of motions and attempts to replicate them, a process that becomes more efficient as time goes on. Mental conceptualization becomes easier to express physically as mind and body become more aligned and synchronized. Danger lies in getting mired in this replication phase, missing out on the intricacies present in subtle skills. Access to the touch of a master often unlocks this, as certain minutiae cannot be conveyed in words or text. That said, the awareness and sensitivity cultivated by standing practices is an invaluable tool in reaching these higher levels. The secret is simply doing. **Do** the practice, **do** the exploration, **do** the self-analysis. On a surface level it may sound enigmatic, but in actuality, it's grounded in just standing around, being grounded.

DRUNKEN STANDING POST

Stand in a drunken stance (modified empty stance) with a cup-fist guard set, slowing your breath, breathing in and out through your entire being. Your skin breathes. Your palms breathe. Your soles breathe. Each breath intoxicates you as it oxygenates your body.

Hold this position on one side, really observing when the shaking occurs, and where any areas of tension can be found throughout the physical structure. At the same time, explore areas of weakness in your mind that try to tempt you into giving up or luring away your attention. The drunkard is focused on the task at hand. When it's time to switch, step forward into the opposite-side stance, and repeat, seeing how it differs from side to side, moment to moment.

DRUNKEN HANDS

Common to a lot of standing training is the "holding the rice bowl" posture, with the hands held in front at about chest height, hands positioned as though holding a bowl (or some slight variation of this positioning). There are two drunken variations for this.

FIRST: Drunken training is well known for its hallmark cup fist, along with "phoenix eye fists" and "sword charm hands", all of which are used in this practice. For the first method, everything is pretty much the same as standard *zhan zhuang*, but hands are held in different positions as the session progresses. Begin with standard, "bowl holding" hands, then every few minutes, change to the

following: sword charm hands, phoenix-eye fists, cup fists. None of these hand formations are clenched; rather, they are squeezed tightly, then released to find the area of "middle tension" or *fang song*. For instance, with the double cup fists held up in front of you, you'll immediately feel tension where the wrists are bent at 45-degree angles. The tighter the fist, the more the torque in the tendons and fascia that becomes apparent. As a warmup, or quick way to calibrate your current tension levels, tightly squeeze your cup fists before immediately relaxing as much as possible. A clear distinction between extreme tension and relaxation is felt in the fingers, wrists and forearms. Next, tighten again, but this time, relax about "halfway", keeping this range as the level of tension needed. Your hands, wrists, and fingers are still roughly in the cup shape position, but are loose and relaxed. This is your drunken cup-fist standing variation.

As with any new standing practice, start with short intervals, and work your way towards longer stints. While longer sessions can have a purpose in training, such as when doing full-time or intensive courses, a reasonable long-term goal is about 20 minutes each time. Keep in mind, that even short practice periods have merit, and it's better to have many short sessions logged throughout the week instead of one long one. Regularity is key. Observe how the change in fists affects various phenomena as you stand. The actual time holding each position depends upon the practitioner's ability and advancement of skill. For instance, in a 20-minute session, each hand structure would be held for five minutes. Adjust the time proportional time periods accordingly.

SOLE SEARCHING

SECOND: The second method is as above, and is more of a dynamic standing practice. It involves shifting weight on your feet as you do the standing, slowly going in circular patterns. Imagine the soles of your feet as having ridges around the sides, and you move your weight around the entire edges of both feet at the same time. For instance, the weight will be on the heels of both feet at the same time, the toes at the same time, and left foot's inner arch coincides with the right foot's right knife edge. Movement and shifting of weight are rhythmic, slow, and deliberate, and should be observed in terms of balance and overall structural dynamics. This is basically standing, albeit with a swaying and circling momentum to it.

WINE BELLY

This particular methodology begins from a standard *Zhan Zhuang* posture, and requires visualization as attention is directed to the belly. Your body's core must be seen as a hollow bottle or gourd that is about one third full of wine. This imaginary liquid is free to swirl and slosh around, continuously moving with an unbroken momentum. While the sway and motion can change pace from slow to fast and back, the wine never remains still. Feet are kept flat on the ground, with arms and hands held in a conventional way. When starting out, keep the range of motions very subtle, ensuring that other aspects of body structure, mental focus, and breathing are not compromised with the addition of this dynamic. Any action that originates in the wine belly necessitates other appropriate movements in the limbs, as full body connection is imperative; nothing moves independently. Nonetheless, things should be fluid and relaxed. There are many facets to examine with this drill, such as how the large and small joints interact and affect each other. Play around with having one or more joints "lubricated" more than others, seeing how this changes the functions of the apparatus overall. For example, if one (or both) knees are afforded more mobility, how does that impact reactions in the torso and shoulders? If the hips are loosened more, does the swirling wine alter the paths vertically, horizontally, or diagonally? Before taking this exploration tight-loose play into the smaller areas of the body, start with attending to the nine major joints: ankles, knees, hips, wrists, elbows, shoulders, waist, middle *dantian*, & neck.

All of these methods are valuable, and regardless of which you're currently focusing on, the key is just to stand around. This kind of standing will take you places.

DAILY DOSE: Warm up all your major joints before starting, and open your lungs with some deep breathing sets. Start with 2-minute sessions standing in this posture, then work up to more and more time (5, 10, 15, 20 minutes). Cool down with deep breathing, joint movements, and self-massage. Drink warm water after a training interval. Just do.

SWIRLING WINE

"No wine remains still"

by Li Xiaotang

In wine tasting circles, why is it swirled before drinking? The following points describe the reasoning and logic behind the practice of evaluating alcohol in this way, but also speak to why drunken fist fighters include "swirling wine" (envisioning the body as a hollow gourd partly full of wine which circles around, driving and informing the motions of the practitioner) as part of the physical practice of their *gong fu*.

1. **Wine is actually tasted with the nose, and the wide assemblage of floral, herbal, mineral, woodsy, fruit, and earthy flavors are the result of aromatic components sensed in the olfactory structures of the body. Swirling releases the different scents which combine with oxygen, making it easier to be subtlety detected by the nose.**

Our boxing is a high-level skill comprised of multiple years of various training methodologies, which are mnemonically activated by using the cup-fist structures and body mechanics of the drunken stances and motions. As the swirling is activated in the hollow gourd-belly, the wide array of skills are brought alive, resulting in a palette of many subtle skills to draw upon for use in combat.

Swirling readies the body for the infinite reactions required for the

chaos that is fighting.

2. **Swirling neutralizes foul-smelling compounds via oxygenation,
    allowing volatile compounds to dissipate, essentially "clearing"
    the wine of impurities.**

The training necessitates a strong knowledge of both correct

breathing as well as parameters of proper physicality. Body

dynamics created by swirling "grease the gears", allowing for

relaxation and fluidity of motion while under the duress of combat.

Relaxation settles the mind, which in turn settles the body.

Cerebrospinal fluid circulation increases, which helps flush out

waste products from the body and keeps the nervous system tuned

and functioning well. Via swirling, the body is rid of impurities, both

mental and physical.

3. **It's more effective in a wider glass than a narrow one, allowing
    for more surface area, and thus more exposure to oxygen,
    especially helpful with older vintages.**

With more practice, lung capacity becomes more efficient, and the

size of influence increases. In other words, as your skill level goes

up, the ability to affect others' increases proportionally (in a combat and mental sense). Having a smoothly functioning breathing apparatus becomes more and more useful both as one rises in combat ability, and as one ages.

4. **Swirling shows the "legs" of the wine, referring to its viscosity and texture. Dense wines spin more slowly.**

Touching an experienced drunken boxer allows you to feel their speed, heaviness, and aptitude, thus giving a taste of their skill level in a brief instant. There are many tools in an expert *zui quan* player's toolbox, one of which is exploring the varying degrees of "viscosity" one can express.

5. **Appearance: it shows awareness and knowledgeability. Spillage is avoided by keeping the glass on the table, moving it around in circles, keeping the base in contact with the table.**

With more exposure to various practitioners, it becomes easier to spot which have internalized some true, heavy, drunken skills, and which are simply theatrically inclined. As for one's own training, it's important to have strong connection to the ground in order to express power. While drunken does have a huge component of "floating root" and floating *jin*, these are layered upon the solid fundamentals of knowing where the ground is connected to you, and powering

from it in some form. "Spillage" is avoided by having solid
foundations, and knowing one's limits and abilities. Proper *zui quan*
teachings include solid *jibengong* and *qigong* sets to impart proper
"color" and "flavor" the wine.

6. **As for aroma and bouquet: The aroma refers to the pleasing
    smells that come from its character and composition, while the
    bouquet is the smells derived from the winemaking process or
    aging.**

"Aroma" can be seen as school, lineage, and teacher, of which the
character and composition of your training derives, including forms,
weapons, and theories. "Bouquet" is the training methodologies, and
how much time and effort you invest in your practice; it's the actual
"process" of working on where you want to be with your training.
You can have wine of great composition ruined by improper storage
and handling. Work towards having fine wine.

In terms of the discussion of *Jing*, *Qi*, and *Shen*, the swirling of wine
is very applicable, and can be observed in this way:

***Jing*:** Once started, the physical motion and currents within don't
stop, flowing from one motion to the next, creating and conserving

momentum in one's engagements, advances, and retreats. One aspect to training drunken forms / *taolu* is starting and maintaining this swirling flow throughout.

Qi: Breath is continuous and unbroken, as the holding of breath pairs with undue tension, inhibiting the drunkard's loose physicality. Smooth and continuous as not to spill the wine, breathing is the connection and conduit between the physical and mental states. Calm breathing softens the mind, which in turn relaxes the body's tension. This is the pivotal relationship between the body and mind, and the mind and spirit.

Shen: Full expression of *Jing* and *Qi* in harmony, demonstrated by engaging in correct *Zui Quan* that is not performative or haphazard. It's an immersion in the *quan* that reflects full effort, and all of the "self", only achievable through continuous practice. It's another aspect is the polished self that develops from unbroken *gong fu* practice over many years, shown in the dedication and concerted effort that leads to natural body connection and fortitude. Pushing through stagnation and overcoming obstacles in ones' life and training reflect in how your *Shen* is ultimately expressed.

SOME ICE WITH YOUR DRINKS

Recuperative temperature extremes

by Xu He Jie

If you've yet to explore the glorious benefits of hot and cold springs, you're in for a treat. Having access to natural hot springs has been one of the easiest and best ways to recover from intensive training sessions, and has never let me down. Just when I thought sitting in a naturally hot pool couldn't get any better, I was introduced to a venue that also had natural cold pools. The two of these in tandem are quite possibly the simplest form of recovery magic one could ever find.

My first exposure to this was when my training partner at the time suggested going to the local natural hot spring after a particularly intense week of practice. Sitting in the geothermically heated water made for instant relaxation, and you could feel it penetrating into the deepest parts of sore musculature. Great.

Steam rising from the large outdoor pools in the early evening somewhat obscured vision, so it was easy to overlook the slightly smaller pool off to the side. Once noticed, we had to check it out, discovering that it was as icy as our current pool was hot. Best not to prolong the discomfort, so we entered quickly, shivering and feeling everything constrict. Breathing had to be consciously drawn in deeply, countering the reflex to pant shallowly and conserve heat. Just as the heat had sunk into the recesses of sore anatomy, the cold penetrated into our very cores. Sitting in this frigid water was itself a form of meditation, as time slowed down and sensations and awareness heightened. Natural survival mechanisms dialed up as a hypothermic sensation settled in. When it felt unbearable – truly unbearable – we'd remain for another slow ten count.

Immediately returning to the steaming hot pool flooded the nervous system with equally intense sensations, but it felt much more medicinal to thaw out like this. Wash, rinse, repeat; this pattern was repeated several times.

Extreme contrast from these two polarized environments really highlighted the spectrum of change one experiences. Heat relaxes, softens and expands, while the cold tightens, hardens, and constricts, and the tangible change from one to the other offered a tremendous opportunity to observe one's own body and mind if conscientious about it. The nervous system settles, circulation increases like no other therapy can imitate, sections of the body requiring massage or liniment make themselves aware, meridians and all systems of the body feel "reset", tuned, and rejuvenated. Magic.

Never do I sleep as well as after one of these hot-cold spring recovery sessions, and physical recovery from training is undeniably faster. *Gong fu* training is hard on the body, so there's definitely benefit to having some heat and ice to go along with your drunken ways.

STAGGERING ALONG PATHWAYS
Rub Yourself Down After Practice: *An Mo*
from discussions with Huang Dekui

The exercises contained in *gong fu* practice invigorate the meridians of the body, wringing and massaging the organs, washing them with blood, providing oxygenation and nourishment, and cleansing waste. Simplifying the movement pathways of every form and *qigong / neigong* set withing a curriculum, there are effectively only three directional planes of motion: vertical, horizontal, and diagonal. A full body strategy covers all of these pathways in various capacities, including strength, flexion, relaxation, endurance / stamina, breath, and so on. If the meridians of the body are seen as physical, connected structures rather than energy distribution conduits, it becomes easy to visualize how one can exercise these portions of the body and keep them healthy and toned.

Drunken Fist warms up the body, then takes it through all of these parameters to various extremes, ultimately seeing the meridians of the body stimulated and maintained, tuned and harmonized. Once the body is loose and the energy is flowing, exercises like sloshing, rocking and swaying become both easier and more effective. Water flows more readily through a waterway unimpeded by sediment and debris.

"Flowing water does not putrefy." Regular activity maintains health.

Martial arts are systems comprised of various tools to augment wellness, which includes meditation, diet, herbal tonics, and massage. This is what keeps the water flowing, preventing staleness and decay. Necessary components of balancing this system are stretching and massage, often overlooked but just as vital for keeping the machine optimized. While many "complete" martial regimens include a deliberate and systematic stretching component, it's equally valuable but less common to include self-massage into one's routine.

Strictly speaking, it's not necessary to have a deep understanding of traditional medicine and acupuncture points in order to do martial arts, or to even reap benefits from such practices. However, increasing familiarity with such things – even on a cursory level – adds a greater intricacy to your studies. Becoming acquainted with some of the major acupuncture points and meridians throughout the body is a useful way of establishing a common vernacular among various martial stylists, and offers further avenues for study, if so interested. At the very least, it answers the question as to "why" such massages are performed in a certain way or location: certain meridians and acupuncture points offer more efficient means of healing and recovery.

Within your lineage, an experienced teacher will have an established massage routine to complement your martial training. All massage methods will adhere to the same general goals and premises, so given the absence of such a resource, you can, at the very least, add some of your own elements of self-massage. Keep in mind that established ways have been tried and tested for long

periods of time over multitudes of people, so there is wisdom in heeding these methodologies.

WHY?

Post-kung fu massage is ultimately about expediting the healing process after a workout. The various techniques employed increase circulation and remove areas of stagnation, as well as build up 衛氣 (*wei qi* / protective *qi*). Any bruising or swollen areas can be flushed with blood, helping to shorten the time period one is under duress from pain or discomfort. Of course, this is done very carefully and mindfully, which helps the practitioner in discerning the functions of one's own body and developing ways of self-diagnosis. Certain stretching or *qigong* components added into the routine are for increasing circulation to organs, and rebalancing the system as a whole. Not only do such techniques help with bringing the mind into the body, they also develop one's own healing capacity, as you can learn to massage others and experience their situations first-hand. Of course, for the more combatively inclined, having a better working knowledge of anatomy definitely helps with fighting abilities.

TECHNIQUES

For starters, there are specific techniques used to achieve desired results, as well as those that are best applied to certain areas of the body. Generally speaking, start from the top of the head and work downwards, and motions are from the center of the body outwards to the sides. Calm yourself by leading your intention down and outwards. As your knowledge progresses, you'll see that such massage routines follow very deliberate pathways in circular motions, using specific "tools" for the distinct tasks and results. For drunken boxers, part of our aim is to "sober up" after intense sessions of "inebriation", hence the focus on calming, centering, and restorative measures.

The "tools" you'll include in your massage repertoire are common to most practitioners, and can be easily researched: pressing, rubbing, pushing, gripping, cupping (rounded palm strikes), slapping (flat palm strikes), striking (fists), pecking (crane beak), chopping (hand ridge penetration strikes), shaking, vibrating, rolling, filing (friction & heat), pulling / traction, tracing (light touch), and combing (fingertips), among possible others. While some of these methods are intuitive, others require a bit more refinement and subtlety;

however, all of them primarily stimulate circulation and clear stagnancy, increasing or dissipating heat as needed. Each will employ different parts of the massage-giver's own anatomy, using fingertips, fingers, knuckles, palms, palm ridges, fists, forearms, or elbows, depending on the type of technique, purpose, or desired intensity.

For instance, "pressing" refers to perpendicular pressure of varying degrees into the receiver's body, which can be meted out using fingertips, fingers, thumbs, palms, fists, forearms, or elbows. Such a technique can be exploratory to a range of depths in order to seek areas of tension, or it can be to relax a certain area, spreading out fluids and accumulated acids. Other techniques such as cupping or slapping are more percussive in nature, and need to be properly adjusted and regulated as not to inflict damage to an area.

SELF-MASSAGE PATTERN

It should be noted that many traditional methods of therapeutic physical treatments include similar approaches to acupressure, palpation, rhythm, and patterns of meridian stimulation. Arrangements may differ, but the logic is relatively constant, with techniques ranging from subtle to quite rigorous.

For our purposes, begin with the head and neck, before moving downwards to the chest, limbs and torso. Particularly when new to the procedures, pay attention to areas on the head and face. As *zui quan* practitioners, familiarization with the continuum of relaxation is paramount, and it's often surprising to see how much tension builds up in areas of the head. The bridge of the nose by the eye sockets is one such place, as are the temples and occipital regions. Working these areas and loosening the neck also greatly correlates with mental relaxation, which cascades downwards as you work along the rest of the body. Rub palms together to create friction and generate heat, placing them over the eyes, then work on specific areas, leading energy downwards to the torso.

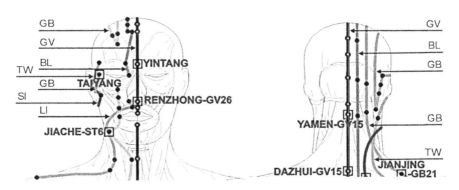

Work on the chest, arms, hands, legs, feet, and stomach / abdomen. Lying face up, you can use your hands to gently massage your internal organs, as they independently need proper circulation and attention, along with finding flow and harmony among them as a whole system. The intestines, liver, stomach, spleen, and gall bladder are in the front of the body and can be treated together, methodically rubbing these areas in a circular fashion.

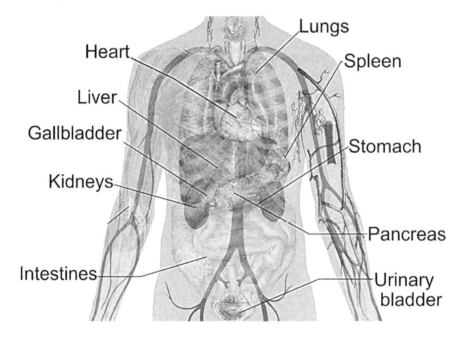

Kidneys are considered very important in Chinese medicine, healing, and martial *qigong* practices, so there are often distinct and purposeful attention paid to them. One obvious way is gently tapping them or rubbing them for a period of time to generate heat in the area, while other approaches include stimulation of the kidney meridian at key points throughout the body. For example, the *yongquan* point at the center of the foot stimulates and regulates the kidneys, so treating

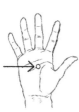

this area is beneficial. While seated, rub palms together to warm the *laogong* points in the center of the hand, placing them directly on the *yongquan* point on the soles of both feet on their respective sides. While doing so, keep your mind focused on your kidneys, drawing attention to and observing sensations in that area of your back.

Any breathing / *qigong* patterns to accompany self-massage should stretch the torso and spine, without rigorous musculature involved. As a calming period, this should include gentle forms of *qigong* that twist, stretch, and lightly stimulate the trunk of the body, but nothing overly strenuous.

Now, will your massage sets work if you're unaware of which pressure points you're stimulating? Yes. One student was absolutely consistent with his post-practice massage, and did not know any of these "mystical energetic theories" or acupuncture points. He achieved much better results than others who were content on memorizing the organs and meridian points, the latter only sporadically doing massage and essentially keeping the concepts academic in nature. As with any *gong fu*, it's easy to lose the forest for the trees. Consistent hard work and application will take you much further than theorizing something to death. "Don't say: do", is the mantra. That said, it's not detrimental to deepen your understanding either; keep things in balance. Learn from a teacher whenever possible, and continue the practice! Follow the established ways and lineages, while also being very attentive to understanding your own physical and energetic body. Depth of understanding is a byproduct of regular, persistent practice.

DAILY DOSE: Set a timer at the end of your workout, beginning with only five minutes. If you exceed that, great. Keep this as the bare minimum, as vital to your martial progress as any of your *gong fu*. You'll likely go beyond this, as the immediate benefits reveal themselves quite quickly.

SHEN

RAISE YOUR SPIRITS

SHEN

It's usually best to relegate concepts and details of the *shen* to the category of "peripheral benefits" rather than something that we define and chase. The contradiction of trying to define something intangible with concrete terms and sensations results in them being further pushed away. Fortunately, by the time one reaches higher levels, illusory concepts and desires for "quick fixes" and "speedy progress" have all but burned away with the bravado of youth. The hard work is done, but the harder work is still to come. Difficulty is found in continuing the practice and finding the drive to do so. This phase requires even more work.

Advanced *gongfu* balances *yi* (intent), *qi* (breath), and *li* (power), demonstrated by a supple structure, strong legs, and movements that can release power. Components are used with more subtlety and in a cleverer way, resulting in "brighter" movements, more intention, and appropriate elements of speed, power, and spirals. Linked by the three 丹田 / *dantians*, advanced practice displays parity between 步法 / *bufa* (stepping methods, hip to leg), 手法 / *shoufa* (hand methods, shoulder to fingers), and 身法 / *shenfa* (body methods, 胯 /

kua to head). While both beginner and advanced techniques may have a physical resemblance, the *intent* is markedly different, and can clearly exhibit one's *shen*.

Essentially, a developed *Shen* is the tangible glow one manifests and exudes after years of concerted effort. It's not something quantified, certainly not something bought, and also quite obvious in one who has devoted the time and effort in developing *Jing* and *Qi*. Chasing the *Shen* – this by-product – actually makes it more unattainable, so it's about putting trust in the process, and simply observing the outcomes.

Not Drinking Alone
No One Achieves Greatness Without Others
from discussions with Wei Laoshi

見佛殺佛

"If you meet Buddha on the path, kill him."

Reduced into very basic terms, it's simply cautionary advice: Throughout this harsh journey of life, if you encounter anyone who offers easy answers or external solutions, wholeheartedly reject this temptation, as it's not truth. True strength and insight exist inside *you*. More succinctly: if something is not authentic, avoid it.

How then, does one reconcile this with the equally wise axiom that "no one achieves greatness alone." In fact, the two concepts dovetail nicely, as they both steer towards the idea of the importance of vetting those we spend our precious time with. For no one is this more crucial than those spending countless hours training, honing, and refining a martial art. Pertinent question to ask include, "Are the others here pushing me to be my very best? Are these others focused and supportive? Is there a positivity to what we're doing?" Not every session will be smiles and sunshine, but there is a vital difference between constructive criticism and criticism, hits and punishment.

We can't choose our families, but we can choose our training halls, partners, role models, and goals. We've heard it said that you become the average of the five people you spend the most time with, which is a pretty powerful tonic, if actually considered. Motivations, attitudes, support, and goals can be positive or negative, and we're actually empowered with the choice of which we want. Yes, there will always be elements of fate or circumstance, but overall, this is something to be very cognizant of with your training...and life.

"If you can tell me who your heroes are, I can tell you how you're going to turn out in life"
-Warren Buffett

Rid yourself of the baggage of negativity, and turn your attention to what matters and nurtures who you are, and who you can be. Success is created by a group who contribute their knowledge and efforts towards the attainment of a definite goal or purpose. I've heard one influential teacher advise to "invest in loss."

"Ever tried. Ever failed. No matter. Try again. Fail again. Fail better."
- Samuel Beckett

Trial and error IS the process. Discover your aptitudes and weaknesses, and use your training partners to lessen the latter. Do the same for others, and the fine-tuning becomes symbiotic. Take on the responsibility of doing this, as it ultimately helps you improve as well.

Invest in loss. This doesn't mean giving up and letting your opponent win: it means trying your best and still losing. Seek those better than you, so your best efforts fail. Aim to be the "stupidest in the room." Do it mindfully, so you can observe the mechanisms and processes of your failures, to learn from them. Become humbled by both your shortcomings and proficiencies.

DAILY DOSE: Take calculated risks, and invest in loss. Mindfully, carefully, consistently: seek that edge. Analyze it.

HABITS DETERMINE YOUR *GONG FU*

from discussions with Guo Tian Rui

Everyone wants the famed "black belt", but very few engage the pain and struggle that is required. As a relatively obscure art, a number of people want to master the art of drunken fist....a very select few are truly willing to break down and rebuild all that is necessary for such an achievement. This is not bragging or bravado; this is statistical fact. There are far more martial arts drop-outs than high-level players. Why is this?

One partial answer is that it's a lonely path as you transcend the steep and rugged mountain of mastery. Mental fortitude and tempering are no small part of the training of this physical cultural artifact. I won't say it's "easy" to do the physical training, but it is quite simple: just don't stop. It's a lot easier to quantify the physical: count your push-ups, count your forms, tally your drills, record your hours of sparring.

So, how do we quantify mental fortitude? This is a multi-faceted topic, and there is not one single way to approach this, but one thing to consider is TIME. How much time do you devote to the multiple facets of your chosen art? A simple equation, TIME x training = (roughly) skill improvement.

Relevant reflection and daydreaming are not wasted time, nor are meditation and internal work. In fact, in a busy lifestyle, scheduling such endeavors may be necessary in order to be fruitful. Habits determine your future path. Simple. You'll not meet a successful person who does not have successful habits, so where does that leave you? What do you sacrifice in order to stay on task?

Journal and map out your timetable, make short-, mid- and long-term plans, and adjust them as you progress forward. Thinks of where you seek to be, and then visualize the means to arrive there. I've yet to meet a high-level martial artist who didn't keep a journal or notebook at some point. At a base level, these "maps" should be divided into mental and physical goals, and your time should be scheduled to maximize efficiency towards these ends. A simple question to continually ask yourself is: "Is what I'm doing right now helping my *gong fu*?" Ultimately, it's about asking: Where is your focus?

When you're not doing the physical components of your day, what are you reading and viewing? How are you eating and resting? Who are you interacting with, and how? Are you leveraging current technology to assist improvement, or frittering the seconds away with hollow entertainment and cheap endorphin fixes online? The internet is both a blessing and curse, so using its potential wisely can be a valuable tool. Videos of a plethora of martial arts fights, techniques, history and theories are available online. While it's easy to get lost in an avalanche of useless information or chasing shiny things down rabbit holes, focused investigation can also unearth some educational gems.

After something like strength training workouts, or forms, or sparring, it's useful to set some time aside to reflect and write about what happened. Putting yourself under the microscope as such can help to reveal weaknesses and fortify strengths for future sessions. Self-analysis is also aided by the ability to record video, offering an objective view of your training. Don't fear technology, but harness it wisely.

A famous quote posits that: "Insanity is doing the same thing over and over again and expecting different results." This is very true of your training. If you feel like you've plateaued or you're not where you should be, perhaps it's time to take an honest inventory of your habits. Your focus decides your destination. You have the tools; you just have to use mental fortitude to distill better habits.

DAILY DOSE: Journal, every day, as writing is a powerful tool. Keep stock of both your physical and mental statuses. Recruit and filter the tools of technology carefully.

BEGGING FOR CHANGE
Prioritize what matters
from discussions with Zhou Yuan Hui

Loading up his meagre motorcycle with as many provisions as it would carry, it wasn't uncommon for the youngster to spend days at a time seeking out hermit teachers that were rumored to exist in the far reaches of his country. Young, driven, focused? Yes. Wealthy? Not in the least. Hearing of a potential source of martial knowledge, he knew how precious this could be, as many of the older generation were either dying off, or becoming less willing to spend their remaining time on fair-weather students. While some trips led to dead ends, many others bore fruit, and resulted in a collage of invaluable martial discussions, demonstrations, and connections for these efforts. In his estimation, they were all worthwhile excursions, even the "failures". Why would he go to such great lengths for potential failure? Why would he trade these potential meet-ups for a more substantial paycheck, given that he needed to miss work to do so? Not only was time spent, school studies postponed, and money sacrificed, a social life was also compromised in this quest. From his perspective, this was the only way to excel at the martial arts that embodied his soul. This was my young teacher, years before I had met him.

Much of this was learned later on, long after I had uprooted myself to go and live in another country and train with him, in a sense, making some similar concessions. Work schedules were adjusted to earn enough to pay for living and training, as well as to coincide with class times. This alone showed a level of dedication he could apprehend. This wasn't something demanded of us, but it became easy to see which training partners invested their all, and which others didn't.

Is this meant to be some sort of badge of pride or bragging? Not at all. In fact, every individual will naturally have their own goals, directives, directions, and levels of commitment. However, it *IS* meant to shed light on the self-deception that many people have regarding their own investment in an art. Time and time again, I've heard would-be students approach a teacher, requesting free training, discounted prices, or "only the high-level knowledge". Another variation of this is only randomly showing up for classes, constantly forgetting previously-taught material, or forgetting to pay on time, if at all. These same students loudly profess their willingness to "break their minds and bodies to learn this art", or make claims about how vital such teachings are to their lives, but it's readily apparent where the cognitive dissonance is playing out. Ultimately, you get out what you put in.

Some take it upon themselves, during class time, to practice other arts they have previously learned, or are currently studying elsewhere. Similar to this is making claims of how "that's the same as we do in X art". The point is: these are all different flavor combinations of the same bad taste.

Yes, you're free to practice and learn whatever and however you want, but it should be pointed out that the disconnect between actions and words is very apparent. If you already know so much, why do you need this teacher? If the classes and books are "really great" and important to your development, why are you haggling over the price? Why do you feel your teacher owes you free lessons, free teaching materials, or free books?

I've purchased many martial arts materials over the years: videos, clothing, weapons, weights, pads, liniments, medicines, supplements, books, magazines, courses, private tutorials...the list goes on. In retrospect, there have been many times when the product wasn't good: it wasn't level appropriate for me, it wasn't something I wanted to pursue, the quality could've been better...the list goes on. That being said, it was *ALL* worth it. Had I not spent money on the lackluster seminar, I wouldn't have known what it was or why it wasn't a good fit. If I hadn't purchased some bad books, I wouldn't have the comparative reference to know what constituted poor quality. Personally, my life has been martial arts, so anything thus-related is a good fit for me. It *ALL* has taught me something, and enriched my martial arts journey.

There will always be those who want everything for free. From my vantage, if something is valuable to you, you'll find a way to invest in it, without de-valuing the efforts of the teacher. Improve yourself; don't expect the world to lower its standards to yours.

DAILY DOSE: Buy things that you value, and that add to your martial arts skills or purview. In your life's overall story arc, the price is worth it. Life is short, so invest in the things that you value. You really do get out what you put in.

COMING UP EMPTY - HANDED
Fill your hands, organize your mind

from discussions with Zhou Yuan Hui

A very "old-school" approach to teaching and training, it was necessary to assist with cleaning up the training area before and after training, done so with a cloth in hand, duck-walking around the vast room, wiping the floor as we went. It was conditioning, hygiene, discipline, and mental focus, all rolled into one simple pursuit. Being "present" during cleaning is a form of high-level meditation. From this cleaning of the training hall habit sprang the adage about "never arriving with empty hands". Our teacher made it clear that one was never to arrive anywhere with empty hands. What was he referring to? First, he made sure we always had a bucket of hot soapy water and a cleaning cloth when we came into the hall, but there was obviously more to it.

"Anytime I went to my teacher's house to learn, I brought him a small gift of fruit, or a drink. If I had no money, I carried in his newspaper from the front stoop. When I left for the day, I emptied the waste basket, and carried out any trash to the curb." Similar anecdotes were repeated over the course of our training, each time revealing other subtle details. What was very clear, was that this precept was quite important for our teacher, and was something that needed to be passed on to us.

This habit carried over to entering and leaving rooms: clearing away dishes, holding a broom, refilling the kettle. What I mean is, this wasn't just servitude or some sort of theater to display only in front of the master; no – we did this in our own rooms, our own kitchens, and in our own lives. It kept things mindful; you would never aimlessly wander into another room, or pace about without purpose, as there is always something to attend to. "Move like you have a purpose!" Living areas became tidier and clean, organically. There wasn't a frantic, compulsive element to it; rather, it was a natural evolution into a comfortable pristineness.

Martial training can be done in multiple facets of one's life, and this is just one further extension of this concept. While it initially seems like only a physical endeavor, it's easy to notice how this quickly ties into maintaining an unfettered mind. There are now many scientific studies that support the claim that a cluttered living space correlates with increased anxiety and other negative mental issues. This is not just fanciful mysticism – cleaning your surroundings also cleans your mind. Keep your hands full, as it truly helps to clear your mind.

DAILY DOSE: Don't leave a room empty-handed. Don't arrive somewhere without bringing something. Make your comings and goings purposeful.

LET'S FIGHT, LET'S PLAY
Fighting mindsets
by Ma Hao Xing & Wang Kunshan

It should be reiterated that training drunken fist *gong fu* has nothing to do with actually ingesting alcohol. The actual "drunkenness" is a combination of theatrics, extreme relaxation, high-level martial skill, and perhaps even feeling inebriated by the endorphins and energy one experiences while expressing *gong fu* in a flow state: being fully immersed and involved in energized focus, feeling the enjoyment of the *zui quan* itself. In fact, one of the core mindsets used when fighting with drunken fist is being playful: you're not actually "fighting" while using these methods, you're "playing", as you would with an object or a friend.

By and large, movement is driven from the central cog of the body that is lower *dantian*, and expresses outwardly via the outer framework that is the body and limbs, thereby maintaining a very solid and sludgy structure. Some have described it as like being hit with a bag of wet, viscous clay. Such movement is initiated when the opponent sets things off, inadvertently creating the cascading waves of motion that express as various strikes, evasions, and counters, like swirling wine rising up and receding. Part of this movement training that encompasses drunken fist is utilization of unusual tempos, which range from slow and messy looking to fast and vibrational. Staggered cadences help give the illusion of incorrect speeds and distances, which is often what people refer to as the "deception" of this fist method. Opponents who are up against such techniques can feel disoriented by the distance / power / timing illusions, ironically, somewhat feeling drunk themselves.

Before we put the cart before the horse, or the theatrics before the drunkard, it's beneficial to have a means of learning this. For this, we'll play a game called "keep the cup". Most effectively trained with another person equally committed to the *zui quan* ways, the idea is to have an object, such as a teacup, and to keep it away from the other person. In the interest of safety, a plastic object without sharp edges makes for fewer injuries and accidents. The mindset is of a drunk who craves another drink, and covets the contents of the wine cup for himself. While trying to retrieve the cup and keep it away from the other player, things are kept playful. When one plays, one relaxes.

As described in the book *"The Path of Drunken Boxing"*:

Players with high levels of skill lack both fear and ego, as there is an inherent confidence in what they practice. [This type of kung fu practitioner] displays such qualities in a playful nature, with the opponent as a "toy" or object. When one plays, one relaxes.

Throughout the process of maintaining possession of your lovely cup of wine, anything that tries to hinder the drinking process gets swatted aside, pushed, poked, swept, leaned on, rolled over, and any other action that keeps the alcohol flowing. The flow is in movements, not stopping and starting, but maintaining continuous momentum once instigated by your training partner, who also yearns for the drink. Make it your goal to roll, fall, trip, stagger, and play as much as possible, all the while keeping control of the object. Do not fear the engagement and crossing of hands, simply see it as a game. Don't simply keep away from the opponent, offer him "drinks" in the form of strikes, clinches, locks, and throws – all playfully executed under the guise of "sharing" a sip...only a sip.

"Feign madness but keep your balance."
The Thirty-Six Stratagems / 三十六計

DAILY DOSE: Start slow, paying attention to flow and relaxation. If you lose the cup, seek it out. If you have the cup, keep it safe. Strikes, kicks, and any other "fighting" are incidental movements as you "enjoy" the drunken state and move through space.

BEING THE CRUELEST DRUNK YOU CAN
Controlling the Violence Diminishes It

If you're unable to mete out violence, you will absolutely be a victim to someone else who can. It was once said, "Prepare your army, or be prepared for someone else's", which is another take on the same concept. No one takes you seriously if you're "nice", which is the incongruity of such an orientation. Being relegated to the category of "harmless" does nothing for you, your community, your training brethren, or anything else that you hold dear, and why is this? Lacking the potential to inflict harm renders you useless at negotiations and leveraging situations, and leaves you intrinsically weak and naïve. The higher the potential danger you can dispense, the more respect you're afforded, which necessarily leads to heightened confidence and control. This is not a directive to seek out violence or a condoning of bully behavior; rather, it's an explanation of the reality that having the *capacity* for violence is a necessity for keeping such things at bay. It does not mean being callous or cruel, it's the potentiality of using your teeth when needed to navigate back to a situational balance or control. Deterrence means being peaceful and avoiding fights as much as reasonable, but having the controlled and confident competency should the necessity arise. True strength and confidence emerge from having this facility, and allow for dominance of a given scenario, which is how one fundamentally achieves peace. Some schools label this as "the integration of the shadow" – knowing humanity's capacity for evil, seeing it in yourself, and then being able to channel and control it. Fighters refer to the "tide of battle" during the throes of combat, wherein one combatant achieves the upper hand over the other. While strategy and luck indeed play a role, the overall determinant of this control goes to the player with the ability to be more aggressive.

At the stage that one is ready to use Drunken Fist, or any other high-level martial art, baseline competencies must be in place which allow for one to traverse the violent terrain that is combat. An opponent must respect your skill, but before that, you must respect and trust your own abilities. Reaching this level comes from dedicated practice and hours of concerted effort, challenges and pushed limits, sharpening the blade that is your *gong fu*. Discover your potential for violence, forge it, enhance it, then keep it under control. Don't be harmless. Don't be "nice". Don't be weak. It's a disservice to all when you are. Use your tools for betterment.

居安思危

"While living in peace, consider danger."
The more you sweat during peacetime, the less you bleed during war.

That said, one can't just "choose" to be exceptionally skilled. The "choice" aspect entails opting to keep on training, and choosing the best means and mindset to do so. We're in the unique position of being the thing that initiates and controls the transformation, but also the object that transforms. Choose to eliminate poor habits and mindsets, as well as people who amplify such behaviors. There is nothing but adversity ahead, but you can determine the flavor of that struggle. A well-known quote with tremendous truth to it is: "The pain of self-discipline will never be as great as the pain of regret."

Challenging what's outside of your conceptual structure is a substantial component of authentic drunken boxing skills. Bending established rules is what leads to attaining the highest skills in *zui quan*. Overcoming preconceptions and misperceptions of the training and results is often the most difficult aspect. Seeing it through to end-points is what leads to unrealized potential, just as failure and failing are tools of growth if reflected upon. Self-flagellation should not come from mistakes; mistakes can help to find meaning and to see the world more clearly. Any good *gongfu* practice is built upon small, discernable components, and that's where analysis should begin. On the plus side, this makes things easier. Find the weakest points in your foundations, and rebuild.

知己知彼百戰不殆

"Know yourself and your enemy, and you'll not be defeated in battle."

Sun Zi, The Art of War

THE FINEST WhINE

水涨船高

"A rising tide lifts all boats"

It's incredibly easy nowadays to find reasons and excuses to not excel at something as challenging as martial arts, especially one as distinct and complex as *zui quan*. One training partner referred to this as *"fine whine"*: the craft and expertise of investing more time at *complaining* rather than *training*. Achieving high-level aptitude necessarily requires a high-degree of self-accountability. This is not self-blame; this is not self-deprecation. This is objectively approaching training in order to reap benefit from all situations, even (and especially) less-than-ideal ones. Any further *sour grapes* is on you.

DAILY DOSE: Be the rising tide. Train *with, for,* and *as* the best.

TRAIN *WITH* THE BEST

"Best" does not always refer to a world champion; it can mean the most appropriate partner for the task at hand. Granted, there are times when there is great utility to being the "worst one in the room", but this should also be balanced with times of being able to dominate an adversary. The problem is, we often get attracted to, and mired in, one of these paradigms. Find ways to learn from whomever you are training with, in a way that pushes you to exceed your boundaries. Even if your available training partner is seemingly terrible, the challenge is readjusting your lens to objectively find ways to reap benefit from the situation.

TRAIN *FOR* THE BEST

Regardless of training goals and focus, one should train as though they're going to be pitted against the highest level of adversary. Increase the quality of the time spent training, mapping out your path: where it has been, where it is, where it's headed to. Maintaining a journal of the training venture is invaluable. Progress and reaching higher levels require pushing boundaries and awareness. Does the intensity of your workout approach match your opponents'? If matched with a kickboxer, does your stamina hold up, or is it laughable? If set against a Taiji player, is your structure and relaxation reasonable? When confronted with a grappler, is your proprioception and technique sufficient to clinch up and be competent on the ground? Keep high standards for the physical confrontation aspect of the art, but also for mental components and health. This chosen art is one with many facets, all of which must be attended to and nurtured as some point.

TRAIN *AS* THE BEST

There is a responsibility to represent your art as best as possible, as it's ultimately a reflection of who *you* are. This is your personality, expression, and abilities being shown. Why be half-hearted, when there is always a new, improved, level to reach? This is certainly not about ego, and in fact, should be the opposite.

At the end of the day, the only one accountable for your level and quality of training is *you*. A great deal of being a high-level practitioner is *maintenance*: maintaining what you've strived for, and honing it to nuanced improvement. No one else can hold you to a high standard, or really push you to improve. This is a personal endeavor, only driven by and achieved by *you*. Be the best you.

EIGHT IMMORTALS CROSS THE SEA
The *Shen* of Being an Immortal
by Zhang Jing Fa

A massive amount of information exists referencing the famed Daoist Eight Immortals: books, stories, dramatic enactments, historical tomes, films, and songs, some good, some bad, some mediocre. With few drawbacks to continually enhancing one's knowledge on a subject, it never hurts to explore more of these channels in the quest for expanding martial pursuits. As other writings in this text have done, the goal is to bridge the theoretical and intellectual aspects of the culture with tangible training approaches to *zui quan*.

Drawing from the teachings I've had access to, the learning of drunken fist is truly only imparted once one has higher level education in mainstream methods. Similar frameworks have been encountered in other lineages as well; in essence, drunken boxing methods are reserved for "advanced" or "committed" practitioners. As an extension of this, the layering and integration of the Eight Immortals' mindsets are considered to be an even further level after this. The logic is sound: you can't build solid structures without strong foundations.

So, why hide the "secrets" like this, in an art that's clearly fading into obscurity? Traditions, paranoia, and secrecy aside, it really distills down to *readiness*. Even if clearly shown or told how something should be done, is the receiver truly *ready* for it? In order to lift exceedingly heavy objects repeatedly, it's something that has to be worked up to gradually and systematically. A higher-level martial art is no different. Iron palm, iron shirt, meditation, lengthy forms: all require preparation and *readiness*.

Once, you're ready, then what? From a strictly practical viewpoint, are the Eight Immortals archetypes simply a means of categorization? Imagine having a fighting system that needed codifying and organization in order to aid with teaching and transmission. Something would be needed to exemplify legwork, grappling, *qin na*, *shuai jiao*, power, timing, striking, clinching, and so on. What better way to do this than to ascribe such qualities to the famed Drunken Immortals of cultural lore? Immediately, the utility becomes obvious, and something that is not unique to drunken boxing. Numerology has played a large role in Chinese cultural traditions since time immemorial, so the cultural overlap with systemizing combat methods is nothing new. Countless other martial arts have been juxtaposed over cultural artifacts as well: *Taiji Quan, Bagua Zhang, Xingyi Quan, Shaolin*. It's just part of the package.

"The Eight Immortals Cross the Sea, Each Displays Celestial Powers"

However, there is more to the use of the *Ba Xian* than just a simple tool for grouping techniques. The Eight Immortals Cross the Sea (八仙過海; bā xiān guò hǎi) is a tale describing the group of Immortals journeying to attend an important conference, at which point they encounter an ocean that must be crossed. Rather than riding the clouds as a means to navigate past the obstacle as Immortals would commonly do, Lü Dongbin suggests that each of them utilize their distinct abilities in order to get across. Subsequently, the proverb shown above describes a scenario in which each individual demonstrates unique proficiency or talent in order to achieve success with a shared objective.

In similar fashion, the techniques, skills, and abilities gleaned from training the archetypal mindsets and fighting methods of each of the Eight Drunken Immortals synergize to result in a formidable and well-rounded combat system. The logic is, where one Immortal's approach may be lacking in a certain area, the deficiency is compensated for by aptitudes of another. For instance, while *He Xian Gu* may not be renowned for kicks, *Zhang Guo Lao* trains in footwork and kicking variations to make up for this.

A theoretical approach to this is not distinct to the Drunken Eight Immortals gong fu training, as other lineages and systems describe a similar rationale. Why have multiple different animal styles? Why have different palm changes? Why have different elements? More modern combat adaptations include being able to fight while standing, clinched, or on the ground. These are all similar answers to the same problems.

Nevertheless, things get a bit more esoteric when you start to require different *mindsets* in order to execute techniques appropriately, which is likely another reason why this level of the training is left until much later in the curriculum. Integrating and expressing the *Shen* of a given Immortal in order to accomplish a technique correctly necessitates more than just physical implementation of an attack or counter. Knowing the characteristics of each, the next iteration is figuring out how that Immortal would execute a technique. How would *Li Tie Guai*'s kicks differ from that of *Cao Guo Jiu*, for example? It's at this stage that the focus really becomes about *quality* over *quantity*. Why do masters of any training system worth its salt still practice the exact same *jibengong* as those done by a rank beginner? On a very surface level, the gross motor movements may appear to follow similar parameters, but the motions of the master are of a completely different quality than that of the students. Requiring students to utilize distinct mindsets to execute techniques necessitates exploring a spectrum of quality in one's training, essentially codifying a philosophy of level and stage training. The subtle qualities of these combat skills are imparted by your teacher via instruction, correction and contact, but the foundational understanding of each Immortal can be established by doing research on the topic. A general starting point includes learning the key words for each, which can be used to finish the statement: "This Immortal's techniques feel quite X."

While legends and stories should be studied in order to add nuance and depth to interpretation of each *Ba Xian*, the aim of this text is training. Rather than expound upon the lore and tales of each of the *Xian*, the following offer training suggestions and key words to explore in order to replicate certain "feelings" associated with the different archetypes.

何仙姑 He Xian Gu – Female and soft, which quickly changes to hard; sharp and pointed. Stepping is quick and grounded, keeps obvious boundaries. Good expressions of upwards and downwards force; splitting. Lots of close fighting, so practice this range and effectively extricating yourself from it.

Key words: 撞擊力 (zhuàng jí lì, "colliding force"), cunning, cutting, flick-y, evasive, quick, controlling

曹國舅 Cao Guo Jiu – Strong, connected, and solid. Any bodywork practices that enhance core strength, particularly with oblique connections between left and right sides. Bridging, closing distances, and lots of *shuai jiao* methods, with focus on quite destructive and punishing takedowns.

Key words: 發力 (fā lì: "expressing power"), powerful, punishing

鐘離權 Zhong Li Quan – Well-based, very grounded. Smothering, with *shuai jiao* and the types of *qin na* skills that involve air and blood seals (choking and strangling). Extremely adept at crushing structure and stealing one's balance with controlling takedowns. A soldier's approach to combat, efficiently ending confrontations decisively.

Key words: 螺旋力 (luó xuán lì: "spiraling or drilling force"), heavy, solid, fluid, snake-like, 動如江河 (dòng rú jiāng hé: "fluid like a river")

韓湘子 Han Xian Zi – Grip strength and *qin na* skills are most affiliated with this immortal, the flautist. Evasive and twitchy means being able to bob, weave and slip strikes, as well as properly execute height changes, done in a showy way. Clinching ability is a must, which incorporates weight drops, joint manipulations, and directional changes. Feints and timing changes overlap well with Han Xiang Zi approaches, allowing for *qin na* setups.

Key words: methodical, precise, changeable, sweeping motions punctuated with 振動力 (zhèn dòng lì: "vibrational force"), evasive.

藍采和 **Lan Cai He** – Confident, relaxed and playful are words that encompass this childlike immortal's archetype, as well as being elusive (both in terms of physical movement and being hard to "read"). Quite "sticky" while at close ranges, the idea is to inflict damage while "playing" with an adversary. Practice should include lots of height changes, timing variance, bridging, and exploration of "body quality" of motion (*shenfa*). Learn to remain relaxed and keep continuous momentum while tumbling around on the ground.

Key words: 波浪勁 (bō làng jìn: "spinal wave energy"), relaxed, rhythmic, fearless, playful, 抖勁 (dǒu jìn: "trembling energy"), elusive, unconventional

呂洞賓 **Lü Dong Bin** – Smooth, long, fluid movements are displayed by this immortal. Very keen awareness of lines of attack and defense, just as a master swordsman would be expected to be versed in. These lines are used for crossing limbs and inducing responses to capitalize on. Lots of practice is spent on pinning parts of an opponent's body with adequate pressure and angles. Fueled by strong intent / *yi*, another skill to cultivate is "reading" opponents with "listening" / *ting jin*.

Key words: refined, controlled, skillful, 按勁 (àn jìn, "pressing energy), 挫勁 (cuò jìn, "filing energy"), subtle, concise, 穿透勁 (chuān tòu jìn: "penetrating energy"), efficient.

張果老 **Zhang Guo Lao** – Often depicted riding a magical mule, the takeaway for the martial artist is that time spent strengthening and achieving flexibility in the legs and hips is never wasted; leg work and stepping are vital. A strong, fluid base is necessary for any sort of high-level *gongfu*, so train these qualities in the lower section: feet, ankles, knees, and hips. Embodying a strong base while playing as this immortal means being able to steal this quality away from others, so this character is adept at foot / ankle / leg sweeps, or any method that robs balance. As an "elder" persona, techniques are subtle and efficient, drawing from years of experience and modesty.

Key words: springy, rooted, coiled, 自轉力 (zì zhuǎn lì: "rotational force"), subtle, discreet.

李鐵拐 **Li Tie Guai** – Gripped by wild intensity and madness, there must be solid underlying skill to stoke the fire of frantic attacks of this "crippled" immortal. Danger and skill can be masked by frenetic and relentless displays in this way. Train body connection and springy, malleable hips, as these both add power to defensive and offensive maneuvers. Weaponize your head, shoulders, and elbows, especially if clinched in tightly. Be well-versed in takedowns, particularly tackles that can be brutal to the one on the receiving end. Whether free-movement, clinching or takedowns, ferocity and drive are unmistakable.

Key words: 爆破力 (bào pò lì, "exploding force"), ruthless, fierce, relentless, explosive, erratic, floating / uprooting

Keep in mind, these are just one interpretation of the immortals, as many variations exist depending on region, lineage, teacher, or students. Some are equally as intricate, while others simply have imitative motions in a form or two. Hopefully you find a teacher and school that matches your needs. Nevertheless, a rudimentary base must exist, then one can be taught the specific stylistic ways to express combat as per the lineage. Regardless of school, advanced levels always find the minimal way to move the maximum amount. "Structure without structure" is not for beginners, as this results in building upon nothing. Exuberance and youthful athletic ability will only carry you so far, but you'll ultimately be left with nothing if you haven't internalized *gong*.

"Advanced levels find the minimal way to move the maximum amount."

Put another way: early stages see students using physical muscle strength to achieve ends, whereas the same advanced technique is accomplished with proper *will* and *intent* to guide things. The latter sees the body engaged, full of power, feel soft power flowing throughout, which necessarily requires *time*. Internal arts often refer to the adage of feeling like "steel wrapped in cotton". Naturally, this can be reversed as well – cotton wrapped in steel – one more illustration of *yin-yang* reversal. The catch? This also necessitates *time*. Coupled with the Eight Immortals ideology, this power is explored and expressed in eight particular ways, if you stick to the paths laid out.

Opponents who are up against drunken techniques can feel disoriented by the distance / power / timing illusions, ironically, somewhat feeling drunk themselves. In fact, a critical part of the higher level Drunken Eight Immortals abilities is being able to impart the qualities of the given immortal onto the adversary. An example of this is how the "cripple", *Tie Guai Li*, aims to disable or debilitate an opponent, or the female *He Xian Gu* attempts to weaken a foe, rendering natural weapons useless with elbow strikes to joints, as examples. Effectively, the challenger is left as a "disabled person" or "weaker female", respectively.

Conversely, some of the tactics of the Immortals are to impart qualities *opposite* to what they portray. For instance, the *Lu Dong Bin* archetype displays refinement of subtle skills in terms of balance, angles, power, and distance, yet uses these elements to undermine these abilities in others. As each immortal's combat methodologies become more second nature, the means to impart these qualities does so as well.

> "If you look at some of the earliest photos of martial arts masters, they look animalistic in their postures. Not in an imitative surface way either, but in a primal, dangerous one. Don't pretend to be an animal – you already are one."
>
> - Shifu Neil Ripski

Similarly, don't pretend to be a Drunken Immortal – you already are one. The idea of these immortals distills certain truths into training methodologies. These mythological characters are essentially composites used to approximate human realities and limitations. They're more than human, but not completely without flaws and insufficiencies. In effect, they show that the plot of life is to

overcome limitations, and that wisdom can be discovered in areas

that you have yet to or don't readily want to explore. Paths to true

self-exploration and development – leading to insight and

enlightenment – are seldom traveled by many.

DRUNKEN TIGERS

from discussions with Shifu Neil Ripski

 "The external, the appearance, means nothing without the internal intent, mind, and spirit of the animal [or Immortal]."

 "No matter the style of the art, there is only one art. Natural, spontaneous, and connected. This is what drives the skill level of a practitioner past good and towards great."

 "These yin moments in training are the moments of change, the amorphous cloud where the player's body is manifesting power, structure, and skill while in motion. Dissolving a shape to create another one. Opponents do not fall from postures; they are defeated by movements. After some time, one starts to see there are far more spaces between the movements than there are movements and postures themselves. Names of the postures begin to take on more and more meaning. Less do they refer to the appearance of the end shape, more do they refer to the movement, mind, and spirit of the techniques itself. The *gongfu* resides in the motion not the stillness at its end."

 "You can't let something go until you have picked it up first."

Invitation to Wine
by Li Bai

將進酒

李白

君不見黃河之水天上來，奔流到海不復回。
君不見高堂明鏡悲白髮，朝如青絲暮成雪。
人生得意須盡歡，莫使金樽空對月。
天生我材必有用，千金散盡還復來。
烹羊宰牛且為樂，會須一飲三百杯。
岑夫子，丹丘生，將進酒，杯莫停。
　　與君歌一曲，請君為我傾耳聽。
鐘鼓饌玉不足貴，但願長醉不願醒。
古今聖賢皆寂寞，惟有飲者留其名。
陳王昔時宴平樂，斗酒十千恣歡謔。
主人何為言少錢，徑須沽取對君酌。
　　五花馬，千金裘，
呼兒將出換美酒，與爾同銷萬古愁。

Do you not see the Yellow River come from the sky,
Rushing into the sea and never come back?
Do you not see the mirrors bright in chambers high
Grieve over your snow-white hair though once it was silk-black?
When hopes are won, oh! Drink your fill in high delight,
And never leave your wine-cup empty in moonlight!
Heaven has made us talents, we're not made in vain.
A thousand gold coins spent, more will turn up again.
Kill a cow, cook a sheep and let us merry be,
And drink three hundred cupfuls of wine in high glee!
Dear friends of mine,
Cheer up, cheer up!
I invite you to wine.
Do not put down your cup!
I will sing you a song, please hear,
O hear! Lend me a willing ear!
What difference will rare and costly dishes make?
I only want to get drunk and never to wake.
How many great men were forgotten through the ages?
But great drinkers are more famous than sober sages.
The Prince of Poets feasted in his place at will,
Drank wine at ten thousand a cask and laughed his fill.
A host should not complain of money he is short,
To drink with you I will sell things of any sort.
My fur coat worth a thousand coins of gold
And my flower-dappled horse may be sold
To buy good wine that we may drown the woes age-old

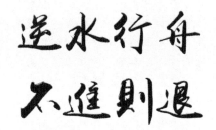

*"Like rowing a boat upstream,
if you stop moving forward, you'll drift back"*

– Proverb

Keep Training...

Printed in Great Britain
by Amazon

47122842R00145